Better Homes and Gardens®

On·the·Go Cook Book

Our seal assures you that every recipe in *On-the-Go Cook Book*
has been tested in the Better Homes and Gardens® Test Kitchen.
This means that each recipe is practical and reliable,
and meets our high standards of taste appeal.

BETTER HOMES AND GARDENS® BOOKS

Editor: Gerald M. Knox
Art Director: Ernest Shelton
Managing Editor: David A. Kirchner
Copy and Production Editors: James D. Blume, Marsha Jahns,
    Rosanne Weber Mattson, Mary Helen Schiltz

Food and Nutrition Editor: Nancy Byal
Department Head, Cook Books: Sharyl Heiken
Associate Department Heads: Sandra Granseth,
    Rosemary C. Hutchinson, Elizabeth Woolever
Senior Food Editors: Julia Malloy, Marcia Stanley,
    Joyce Trollope
Associate Food Editors: Linda Henry, Mary Major,
    Diana McMillen, Mary Jo Plutt, Maureen Powers,
    Martha Schiel, Linda Foley Woodrum
Recipe Development Editor: Marion Viall
Test Kitchen Director: Sharon Stilwell
Test Kitchen Photo Studio Director: Janet Pittman
Test Kitchen Home Economists: Lynn Blanchard,
    Jean Brekke, Kay Cargill, Marilyn Cornelius,
    Jennifer Darling, Maryellyn Krantz, Lynelle Munn,
    Dianna Nolin, Marge Steenson

Associate Art Directors: Linda Ford Vermie, Neoma Alt West,
    Randall Yontz
Assistant Art Directors: Lynda Haupert, Harijs Priekulis,
    Tom Wegner
Senior Graphic Designers: Jack Murphy, Stan Sams,
    Darla Whipple-Frain
Graphic Designers: Mike Burns, Sally Cooper, Blake Welch,
    Brian Wignall, Kimberly Zarley

Vice President, Editorial Director: Doris Eby
Executive Director, Editorial Services: Duane L. Gregg

President, Book Group: Fred Stines
Director of Publishing: Robert B. Nelson
Vice President, Retail Marketing: Jamie Martin
Vice President, Direct Marketing: Arthur Heydendael

ON-THE-GO COOK BOOK

Editor: Linda Foley Woodrum
Copy and Production Editor: James D. Blume
Graphic Designer: Mike Burns
Electronic Text Processor: Donna Russell
Contributing Photographers:
    Michael Jensen and Sean Fitzgerald
Food Stylists: Therese McDonnell, Janet Pittman,
    Maria Rolandelli

On the cover: *Speedy Taco Salad* (see recipe, page 6)

Contents

Speedy Taco Salad
(see recipe, page 6)

Things Are Looking Up!

Whatever your family situation, with this book as part of your work force, you can say good-bye to mealtime rush hour. In *On-the-Go Cook Book* we lavish you with quick-to-fix recipes (on the table in 30 minutes), recipes that cook all day while you're gone, and others that you can make the night before. You'll even find dishes that kids can start before Mom and Dad get home, plus some terrific breakfast and lunch ideas. So why waste another minute? Bid farewell to kitchen-time overtime.

Speedy Taco Salad

Also pictured on the cover.

Total Time: 30 minutes

1 **pound ground beef** *or* **ground raw turkey**
1 **large onion, chopped**
2 **10-ounce cans tomatoes and green chili peppers**
1 **1¼-ounce package taco seasoning mix**

½ **head lettuce, shredded**
2 **cups shredded cheddar cheese (8 ounces)**
2 **medium tomatoes, chopped**
8 **pitted ripe olives, sliced**
3 **green onions, sliced**
  Dairy sour cream
  Taco sauce
4 **cups tortilla chips**

● In a large skillet cook meat and onion till meat is brown and onion is tender. Drain off fat. Stir in tomatoes and green chili peppers and seasoning mix. Simmer, uncovered, for 8 to 10 minutes or to desired consistency.

● Set out lettuce, cheese, tomatoes, olives, onions, sour cream, and taco sauce. Arrange tortilla chips on 4 dinner plates. Spoon meat mixture over chips. Top meat mixture with desired toppings. Makes 4 servings.

What a time-saver! Family members can assemble their own Mexican masterpieces right at the table.

Ginger-Walnut Chicken

Total Time: 20 minutes

1 **whole large chicken breast, skinned, boned, and halved lengthwise** **Salt** **Pepper**	● Place 1 piece of chicken between 2 pieces of clear plastic wrap. Pound to ¼-inch thickness. Repeat with remaining chicken. Sprinkle with salt and pepper.
1 **tablespoon butter *or* margarine**	● Meanwhile, in a large skillet melt butter or margarine. Brown chicken in hot butter for 4 to 6 minutes or till tender, turning once. Remove from skillet. Keep chicken warm.
2 **teaspoons sugar** 1 **teaspoon cornstarch** ½ **cup orange juice** 1 **teaspoon grated gingerroot** 2 **tablespoons coarsely chopped walnuts***	● Stir together sugar and cornstarch. Stir in orange juice and gingerroot. Add to skillet. Cook and stir till thickened and bubbly. Cook and stir 2 minutes more. Add chicken, turning to coat. Sprinkle with nuts. Makes 2 servings.

If you don't have time to toast the walnuts, don't worry about it. Just use the untoasted ones. You'll still get a nice nutty flavor.

*****Note:** If desired, toast the walnuts by placing them in a single layer on a baking sheet. Bake in a 350° oven for 10 to 15 minutes or till the nuts are toasted.

Or, place 1 cup walnuts in a 2-cup glass measure. Micro-cook, uncovered, on 100% power (high) for 3 minutes, stirring every minute. Cook for 1 to 2 minutes more, stirring every 30 seconds. Let stand 15 minutes. The nuts will continue to toast while standing.

Orange Turkey Tenderloins

Total Time: 30 minutes

1 teaspoon finely shredded
    orange peel
½ cup orange juice
¼ cup water
2 tablespoons dry sherry
2 teaspoons cornstarch
1½ teaspoons instant chicken
    bouillon granules

● For sauce, in a small mixing bowl stir together orange peel, orange juice, water, sherry, cornstarch, and chicken bouillon granules. Set aside.

Let's talk turkey. Fresh turkey breast tenderloins are very lean cuts of white meat that are skinless and boneless. You can expect to find two to four pieces in a one-pound package.

4 fresh turkey breast
    tenderloins (about 1½
    pounds total)
2 tablespoons cooking oil
3 medium carrots, thinly
    sliced

● In a large skillet cook turkey in hot oil for 4 to 5 minutes on each side or till tender. Remove from skillet. Reduce heat to medium. Add carrots to skillet. Cook and stir for 6 to 8 minutes or till tender.

    Push carrots to side of skillet. Stir sauce. Add sauce to skillet. Cook and stir till thickened and bubbly. Return turkey to skillet. Cover and cook about 2 minutes more or till turkey is heated through. Makes 4 servings.

Microwave Method: For sauce, in a 2-cup glass measure stir together orange peel, orange juice, *2 tablespoons* water, sherry, cornstarch, and chicken bouillon granules. Set aside.

    In a 12x7½x2-inch nonmetal baking dish combine turkey, carrots, and 2 tablespoons *water*. (Omit oil.) Micro-cook, covered, on 100% power (high) for 7 to 8 minutes or till turkey and carrots are tender, rearranging turkey pieces after 4 minutes. Drain and set aside.

    Stir sauce. Micro-cook, uncovered, on high for 2 to 4 minutes or till thickened and bubbly, stirring every minute. Serve over turkey and carrots.

Turkey 'n' Fruit Plate

Total Time: 30 minutes

Assorted fresh fruit (banana and kiwi fruit slices, melon balls, *or* pineapple and plum wedges)
Lemon juice
Lettuce leaves

● Wash fruit, if necessary. If using banana slices, dip them in lemon juice to prevent browning. Arrange fruit on 3 lettuce-lined plates.

3 slices cheddar, Colby, *or* Swiss cheese
1 6-ounce package (6 round slices) sliced turkey luncheon meat
½ cup lemon *or* orange yogurt
2 tablespoons mayonnaise *or* salad dressing
1 tablespoon milk
½ teaspoon poppy seed
Breadsticks (optional)

● Cut cheese into strips. Divide cheese strips among turkey slices. Roll turkey slices around cheese strips. Arrange on plates next to fruit.

In a small bowl stir together lemon or orange yogurt, mayonnaise or salad dressing, milk, and poppy seed. Drizzle over fruit and turkey rolls. Serve with breadsticks, if desired. Makes 3 servings.

This recipe makes a refreshing hot weather meal. If your favorite fruit isn't in season, use frozen or drained canned fruit.

Pizza Fish Fillets

Total Time: 20 minutes

2 ½-inch-thick bias-sliced pieces of French bread
Butter *or* margarine
Garlic powder
¼ cup shredded mozzarella cheese (1 ounce)

● Spread bread slices with butter or margarine. Sprinkle lightly with garlic powder. Place on the unheated rack of a broiler pan. Broil 4 inches from the heat for 1 to 2 minutes or till toasted. Sprinkle with cheese. Broil till cheese melts. Remove bread slices from broiler.

Savor the flavor of pizza, but this time with a new twist. Top toasted French bread with mozzarella cheese, tender fish, and pizza sauce.

2 individually frozen fish fillets (about 4 to 5 ounces each)
⅓ cup pizza sauce
¼ cup shredded mozzarella cheese (1 ounce)

● Place frozen fish fillets on rack of broiler pan. Broil fillets about 4 inches from the heat till fish flakes easily with a fork (allow 6 to 9 minutes for each ½ inch of thickness).
   Return toasted bread to broiler rack. Transfer 1 fillet to each slice of bread (see photo, below). Spoon sauce over fish. Sprinkle with cheese. Broil for 1 to 2 minutes more or till sauce is hot and cheese melts. Makes 2 servings.

To assemble, return the toasted French bread to the hot broiler rack. Use a spatula to transfer one fish fillet to each slice of bread.

Vegetable Fish Fillets

Total Time: 25 minutes

½ cup sliced fresh
mushrooms
1 medium carrot, cut into
julienne strips
1 green onion, sliced
1 tablespoon butter *or*
margarine

● In a 10-inch skillet cook mushrooms, carrot, and onion in butter or margarine over medium-high heat for 4 to 5 minutes or till carrots are just crisp-tender. Remove vegetables from skillet with a slotted spoon.

1 11½-ounce package
(4 portions) individually
frozen fish portions
½ of a lemon
⅛ teaspoon garlic powder
Salt
Pepper
1 medium tomato, cut into
8 wedges

● Arrange frozen fish in skillet. Squeeze lemon over fish. Sprinkle with garlic powder, salt, and pepper. Cover and cook over medium heat for 5 minutes. Spoon vegetable mixture over fish. Add tomato wedges. Cover and cook for 2 to 4 minutes more or till fish flakes easily with a fork. Makes 4 servings.

Microwave Method: In a 10x6x2-inch baking dish place mushrooms, carrots, onion, and butter or margarine. Cover with clear plastic wrap; vent by leaving a small area unsealed at the edge of the dish. Micro-cook on 100% power (high) about 3 minutes or till carrots are crisp-tender, stirring once. Remove vegetables and juices from dish. Set aside.

Place frozen fish in baking dish. Squeeze lemon over fish. Sprinkle with salt, pepper, and garlic powder. Cover and cook on high for 4 minutes, turning fillets over and rotating dish after 2 minutes. Spoon vegetable mixture over fish. Top with tomato. Cover and cook about 2 minutes more or till fish flakes easily with a fork. Let stand for 1 minute.

The lemon is known as the fruit with a thousand uses. Put it to good use here with fish and vegetables. If you don't have a fresh lemon, use 1½ tablespoons of bottled lemon juice.

Hurry-Curried Pork and Potatoes

Total Time: 25 minutes

3 medium potatoes (about 1 pound total)	● Scrub potatoes. Cut each potato lengthwise into 6 slices. Cook potato slices in boiling salted water about 10 minutes or till tender; drain. Keep warm.

Potato pinwheels make an attractive base for this creamy pork mixture, but it's just as good spooned over baked potatoes or hot cooked rice.

¾ pound boneless pork, cut into thin bite-size pieces 1 small apple, cored and chopped 1 green onion, sliced 1 to 2 teaspoons curry powder 1 tablespoon cooking oil 1 7¾-ounce can semi-condensed cream of mushroom soup ½ cup dairy sour cream ⅓ cup milk 1 tablespoon snipped parsley	● Meanwhile, in a small skillet cook pork, apple, green onion, and curry powder in hot oil for 3 to 4 minutes or till pork is no longer pink. Stir in soup, sour cream, milk, and parsley. Cook and stir till heated through. *Do not boil.*

Raisins *or* peanuts (optional)	● To serve, arrange potato slices in spoke fashion on 3 dinner plates. Spoon pork mixture over the potatoes (see photo, below). Sprinkle with raisins or peanuts, if desired. Makes 3 servings.

Arrange potato slices in spoke fashion on dinner plates. Spoon the pork mixture over the potatoes.

Sweet 'n' Sour Ham

Total Time: 20 minutes

¼ cup packed brown sugar 1½ teaspoons cornstarch ⅛ teaspoon ground ginger ¼ cup water 2 tablespoons red wine vinegar 2 teaspoons soy sauce	● In a small mixing bowl stir together brown sugar, cornstarch, and ginger. Stir in water, red wine vinegar, and soy sauce. Set aside.
1 ½-pound fully cooked ham slice	● In a medium or large skillet cook ham over medium heat about 5 minutes or till lightly browned, turning once. Remove ham from skillet. Keep warm.
½ cup seedless red *or* green grapes, halved	● Stir cornstarch mixture. Add to skillet. Cook and stir till thickened and bubbly. Cook and stir 1 minute more. Add grapes. Heat through. Serve over ham. Makes 2 servings.

Microwave Method: In a 2-cup glass measure stir together brown sugar, cornstarch, and ginger. Stir in water, vinegar, and soy sauce. Set aside.

Place ham in a 10x6x2-inch nonmetal baking dish. Cover with waxed paper. Micro-cook on 100% power (high) for 1½ minutes. Turn ham over and cook for 1 to 1½ minutes more or till heated through. Keep warm.

Stir cornstarch mixture. Micro-cook, uncovered, on high for 1 to 1½ minutes or till thickened and bubbly, stirring once. Cook for 30 seconds more. Stir in grapes. Serve over ham.

It's not for sweethearts or sourpusses; it's for those who love the tangy blend of red wine vinegar, brown sugar, and spices.

In-a-Flash Frittata

Total Time: 20 minutes

2 small green onions, sliced 1 tablespoon butter *or* margarine	● In an 8-inch oven-going skillet cook green onions in butter or margarine till onion is tender.
6 eggs ¼ cup milk ½ teaspoon Italian seasoning ⅛ teaspoon pepper 2 ounces thinly sliced prosciutto *or* fully cooked ham, chopped	● In a medium mixing bowl beat together eggs, milk, Italian seasoning, and pepper with a rotary beater till frothy. Stir in prosciutto or ham. Pour egg mixture into skillet with onion mixture. Cook over medium heat, lifting edges occasionally to allow uncooked portion to flow underneath. Cook about 4 minutes or till top of egg mixture is almost set.
1 small tomato, chopped ¼ cup shredded mozzarella cheese *or* 2 tablespoons grated Parmesan cheese	● Top egg mixture with tomato. Sprinkle with cheese. Place skillet under broiler about 5 inches from heat. Broil about 2 minutes or till tomato is heated through. Cut into wedges to serve. Makes 3 servings.

A frittata is really just an open-face omelet. This one's brimming with prosciutto (Italian ham), green onions, tomatoes, and cheese.

Use a skillet with sloping sides. It makes for easier removal of the frittata. If you don't have an oven-going skillet, be sure to cover the handle with foil.

Microwave Method: In a 7-inch nonmetal pie plate combine onions and butter or margarine. Micro-cook, uncovered, on 100% power (high) about 2 minutes or till onion is tender.

In a small mixing bowl beat together eggs, milk, Italian seasoning, and pepper with a rotary beater till frothy. Stir in prosciutto or ham. Pour into pie plate with onion mixture. Cook, uncovered, on high for 3 to 4 minutes or till eggs are almost set, pushing cooked portions to center of dish several times.

Top with tomato and sprinkle with cheese. Cook, uncovered, about 30 to 45 seconds more or till tomato is heated through. Let stand 4 to 5 minutes.

Sausage Pilaf

Total Time: 30 minutes

1 medium carrot, sliced ¼ inch thick
1 tablespoon butter *or* margarine
2 teaspoons dried parsley flakes
½ teaspoon instant chicken bouillon granules
½ teaspoon dried oregano, crushed
¼ teaspoon onion powder
⅛ teaspoon garlic powder
⅓ cup bulgur
2 fully cooked Polish sausages (3 to 4 ounces each)

● In a 2-quart saucepan cook carrot in butter or margarine for 3 minutes. Stir in parsley flakes, bouillon granules, oregano, onion powder, garlic powder, and 1 cup *water*. Bring to boiling. Stir in bulgur. Reduce heat. Cover and simmer for 10 minutes.

Diagonally slash the sausages 3 or 4 times. Add sausage to bulgur mixture in saucepan. Cover and simmer about 5 minutes more or till sausage is heated through. Makes 2 servings.

We switched bulgur (precooked cracked wheat) for rice in this pilaf because bulgur has a unique nutty flavor.

Tongue-Tingling Tofu

Total Time: 25 minutes

⅓ cup water
2 tablespoons dry sherry
2 tablespoons soy sauce
2 teaspoons cornstarch
1 teaspoon grated
   gingerroot
1 teaspoon instant chicken
   bouillon granules
¼ teaspoon crushed red
   pepper

● For sauce, in a small mixing bowl stir together water, sherry, soy sauce, cornstarch, gingerroot, bouillon granules, and red pepper. Set aside.

Think of tofu as a sponge. It absorbs the other flavors that it's cooked with. In this case, it soaks up lots of spicy sauce.

¾ cup quick-cooking rice
1 tablespoon cooking oil
1 medium green *or* red
   sweet pepper, cut into
   bite-size pieces
3 green onions, bias-sliced
   into 1-inch pieces

● Prepare rice according to package directions. Meanwhile, preheat a wok or medium skillet over high heat; add cooking oil. Add green or red pepper and onions. Stir-fry about 2 minutes or till vegetables are crisp-tender. Push vegetables from center of wok.

8 ounces tofu (soybean
   curd), cut into ½-inch
   cubes (1½ cups)
½ cup unsalted cashews *or*
   peanuts

● Stir sauce. Add to center of wok. Cook and stir till thickened and bubbly. Cook and stir for 1 minute more. Stir in tofu. Cover and cook for 1 minute. Serve over rice. Sprinkle with nuts. Serves 2.

Tofu Trivia

Move over yogurt, you've got company. Tofu (also known as soybean curd) is a favorite of health-conscious Americans from coast to coast, and it's no wonder. Tofu contains no cholesterol, it's high in protein, and it's low in calories, fat, and carbohydrates. You can eat tofu instead of meat or team it with meat in many of your favorite dishes.

The real beauty of tofu is its versatility. By itself, tofu is bland and high in moisture. But that's exactly why it so deliciously absorbs other flavors. You can boil it, broil it, stir-fry it, bake it, or fry it. Try the recipe Tongue-Tingling Tofu for starters. Then experiment with tofu on your own.

Quick Ranch-Style Eggs

Total Time: 25 minutes

3 6-inch flour tortillas	● Wrap the tortillas in foil and place in a 375° oven for 3 minutes. Remove tortillas from foil and press into three 10- or 15-ounce custard cups (see photo, top right). Bake in a 375° oven for 8 to 10 minutes or till tortillas are crisp.
1 10-ounce can tomatoes and green chili peppers **6 eggs**	● Meanwhile, in a medium skillet bring tomatoes and green chili peppers to boiling; reduce heat. Carefully break eggs into the skillet. Cover and simmer eggs over low heat about 5 minutes or to desired doneness.
¾ cup shredded Monterey Jack cheese (3 ounces)	● Sprinkle *half* of the cheese into the bottoms of the tortilla cups. Carefully spoon 2 eggs, one at a time, into *each* tortilla cup (see photo, bottom right). Spoon tomato mixture into tortilla cups. Sprinkle with remaining cheese. Bake tortilla cups about 2 minutes more or till cheese melts. Makes 3 servings.

To soften the tortillas and prevent cracking, wrap them in foil and heat them for a few minutes in the oven. Remove the tortillas from the foil. Gently push the tortillas into the custard cups.

To assemble, spoon two eggs and some of the tomato mixture into each baked tortilla cup.

Choose-a-Flavor Floats
(see recipe, page 20)

30-Minute Menu

Sit down to this speedy dinner for four a mere half hour after you walk in the door. Dovetailing recipe steps is the key to beating the clock. Just follow our timetable below and you'll come through with flying colors.

MENU

Simple Stuffed Steaks
Steamed broccoli spears
Lettuce wedges with cottage
  cheese and salad dressing
Crackers
Choose-a-Flavor Floats

MENU COUNTDOWN

30 Minutes Ahead

Prepare and broil the Simple Stuffed Steaks. While steaks broil, bring water to boiling for broccoli. Scoop ice cream for Choose-a-Flavor Floats into tall glasses. Place in freezer. Steam broccoli.

5 Minutes Ahead

Cut the lettuce into wedges. Arrange on salad plates. Spoon cottage cheese and salad dressing over lettuce. Place crackers on salad plate.

At Dessert Time

Pour root beer over ice cream in glasses.

Simple Stuffed Steaks
(see recipe, page 20)

Simple Stuffed Steak

Pictured on pages 18–19.

Total Time: 30 minutes

2 ¾- to 1-pound beef top
    loin steaks, cut 1 to
    1½ inches thick
1 small onion, chopped
1 medium carrot, shredded
1 tablespoon butter *or*
    margarine
2 tablespoons snipped
    parsley
¼ teaspoon dried
    basil, crushed
⅛ teaspoon garlic powder
    Dash salt
    Dash pepper

● Cut a deep slit horizontally in each steak to form a pocket. In a small saucepan cook the onion and carrot, covered, in butter or margarine for 2 to 3 minutes or till tender. Stir in parsley, basil, and garlic powder. Spoon mixture into pockets in meat. Secure openings of pockets with wooden skewers or toothpicks. Sprinkle with salt and pepper.

**Simple ingredients.
Simple preparation.
Simply delicious!**

● Place steaks on the unheated rack of a broiler pan. Broil 4 inches from the heat for 6 minutes. Turn meat and broil to desired doneness, allowing 6 to 8 minutes more for medium. Remove skewers or toothpicks. Makes 4 servings.

Choose-a-Flavor Floats

Pictured on pages 18–19.

Total Time: 5 minutes

8 scoops vanilla, chocolate,
    coffee-flavored, butter
    brickle, *or* chocolate-
    swirl ice cream
2 12-ounce cans root beer
    Maraschino cherries
    (optional)

● Put 2 scoops of ice cream into four 12-ounce glasses. Slowly pour root beer over ice cream to fill the glasses. Garnish with cherries, if desired. Serves 4.

We tested each and every variation with pleasure. The coffee ice cream and root beer combination was our favorite.

Lamb-Patty Pitas

Total Time: 25 minutes

¾ cup soft bread crumbs
¼ cup milk
½ teaspoon dried minced onion
¼ teaspoon dry mustard
⅛ teaspoon garlic powder
¾ pound ground lamb

● In a mixing bowl stir together crumbs, milk, onion, mustard, and garlic powder. Add lamb. Mix well. Shape into four ½-inch-thick oval patties.

Place patties on the unheated rack of a broiler pan. Broil 3 to 4 inches from the heat for 4 minutes. Turn and broil to desired doneness, allowing 3 to 5 minutes more for medium.

Who said burgers have to be round? Shape the lamb patties into ovals so they fit easily into the pitas.

1 small cucumber, seeded and finely chopped
½ cup plain yogurt
¼ cup chopped pitted ripe olives
2 teaspoons sesame seed, toasted
4 lettuce leaves
2 6-inch pita bread rounds, halved crosswise

● Meanwhile, combine cucumber, yogurt, olives, and sesame seed. Place lettuce leaves in pita pockets. Spoon some of the cucumber mixture onto lettuce. Place patties in pita pockets. Spoon remaining cucumber mixture over each patty. Makes 4 servings.

Ingredient Substitutes

Oops! You're missing a few ingredients needed for a recipe. Instead of making a mad dash to the grocery store, glance at the list below. There's a good chance you'll find a suitable substitute for what you're missing.

● 1 tablespoon cornstarch..............2 tablespoons flour for thickening
● 1 cup granulated sugar ....1 cup brown sugar or 2 cups sifted powdered sugar
● 2 cups tomato sauce....................¾ cup tomato paste plus 1 cup water
● 1 cup tomato juice.......................½ cup tomato sauce plus ½ cup water
● 1 cup chicken or beef broth ....1 teaspoon instant chicken or beef bouillon granules plus 1 cup water
● 1 small onion ....⅛ teaspoon onion powder or 1 tablespoon dried minced onion
● 1 clove garlic................................⅛ teaspoon garlic powder
● 1 tablespoon fresh snipped herbs ....1 teaspoon dried herbs, crushed
● 1 square (1 ounce) unsweetened chocolate..........3 tablespoons unsweetened cocoa powder plus 1 tablespoon shortening

Raid the Kitchen

Unload the grocery bags and stock your freezer, refrigerator, and cupboards with a variety of work-saving ingredients. Always keep a few of these in the kitchen to make last-minute dinner decisions easier and to streamline the cooking. These are just some of the work savers we used in this cooking-with-what's-on-hand section.

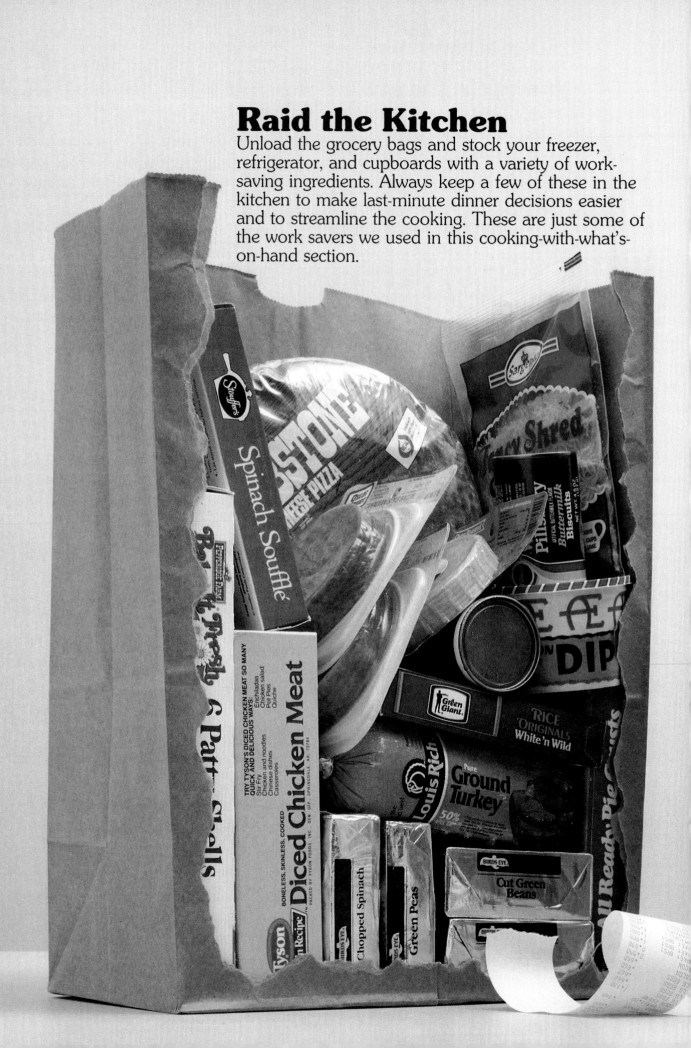

Cheesy Tuna-Vegetable Soup

Total Time: 40 minutes

4	cups (32 ounces) vegetable juice cocktail
1	14½-ounce can beef broth
1	10-ounce package frozen succotash
1	9-ounce package frozen cut green beans
1	cup elbow macaroni
1	teaspoon dried basil, crushed
1	teaspoon Worcestershire sauce
¼	teaspoon ground red pepper

● In a 4½-quart Dutch oven combine vegetable juice cocktail, beef broth, frozen succotash, frozen green beans, macaroni, basil, Worcestershire sauce, and red pepper. Bring to boiling; reduce heat. Cover and simmer for 25 to 30 minutes or till the macaroni and vegetables are tender, stirring frequently.

Open the cupboard and dig into the freezer. That's where you'll find the fixin's for this tummy-warming soup.

1	9¼-ounce can tuna, drained and flaked
1	8-ounce jar cheese spread

● Stir in tuna and cheese till cheese melts and tuna is heated through. Makes 4 or 5 servings.

Quick-Thaw Salad Supper

Total Time: 35 minutes

1	8-ounce bottle creamy cucumber salad dressing
1	10-ounce package frozen long-grain and wild rice
1	10-ounce package frozen peas

● Chill cucumber dressing in the freezer while preparing salad. Thaw rice by placing pouch in a bowl of hot water for 5 minutes, breaking up rice occasionally. (Some chunks will remain.) Thaw peas by placing them in a colander under cold running water for 2 to 3 minutes.

With this recipe, it's easy to do two things at once. Thaw the rice in a bowl of hot water while you rinse the frozen peas in a colander.

4	ounces cheddar *or* Swiss cheese, cubed
2	small apples, cored and sliced
1	7¾-ounce can salmon, drained, flaked, and skin and bones removed

● In a large mixing bowl toss together rice, peas, cheese cubes, and apple slices. Add salmon and toss lightly.

2	cups spinach leaves
½	cup shredded carrot

● Line 4 dinner plates with spinach leaves. Mound salmon mixture on top. Pour dressing over and sprinkle with shredded carrot. Makes 4 servings.

Salmon-Sauced Patty Shells

Total Time: 35 minutes

3 frozen patty shells
1 stalk celery, chopped
2 tablespoons butter *or*
    margarine
2 tablespoons all-purpose
    flour
½ teaspoon dried dillweed
1 cup milk
½ cup shredded American *or*
    process Swiss cheese
    (2 ounces)

● Bake frozen patty shells according to package directions. Meanwhile, in a medium saucepan cook celery in butter or margarine till tender. Stir in flour and dillweed. Add milk all at once. Cook and stir till thickened and bubbly. Cook and stir 1 minute more. Stir in shredded cheese till it melts.

An elegant entrée from convenience foods? You bet!

1 7¾-ounce can salmon,
    drained, flaked, and
    skin and bones removed
1 2½-ounce jar sliced
    mushrooms, drained
2 tablespoons chopped
    pimiento

● Add salmon, mushrooms, and pimiento to the cheese mixture in saucepan. Heat through, stirring occasionally. Keep warm. Place patty shells on individual plates. Spoon salmon mixture into patty shells. Serves 3.

A 9¼-ounce can of tuna makes a great stand-in for the salmon.

Turkey and Stuffing

Total Time: 45 minutes

1 beaten egg 1 cup herb-seasoned stuffing mix, crushed ¼ cup milk 1 pound ground raw turkey 2 tablespoons cooking oil	● In a medium mixing bowl combine egg, stuffing mix, and milk. Add turkey. Mix well. Shape meat mixture into eight 4x1-inch logs. In a large skillet cook meat logs in hot oil till brown, carefully turning frequently. Drain off fat.

1 16-ounce can whole
    cranberry sauce
½ cup dry white wine
2 teaspoons chicken
    bouillon granules
2 cups hot cooked noodles
2 green onions, sliced
	● In a mixing bowl stir together whole cranberry sauce, wine, and chicken bouillon granules. Pour over meat in skillet. Bring to boiling; reduce heat. Cover and simmer about 15 minutes or till meat is done. Uncover and cook about 5 minutes more or till sauce is of desired consistency. Serve over hot cooked noodles. Sprinkle with sliced green onions. Makes 4 servings.

It's not your typical Thanksgiving dinner. It's much quicker! Combine and shape ground turkey and stuffing mix into tasty logs, cook them with a cranberry sauce, then serve them over hot cooked noodles.

Rice-Stuffed Peppers

Preparation: 15 minutes
Baking Time: 40 minutes

½ cup quick-cooking rice ⅓ cup water	● In a small saucepan stir together rice and water. Bring to boiling; remove from heat. Cover and let stand for 5 minutes.

2 medium green peppers
1 beaten egg yolk
½ cup diced Canadian-style
    bacon *or* fully cooked
    ham
½ cup shredded cheddar
    cheese (2 ounces)
⅓ cup chopped unsalted
    peanuts
2 tablespoons catsup
	● Meanwhile, halve peppers lengthwise. Remove seeds and membranes from peppers. Stir together egg yolk, Canadian-style bacon or ham, cheese, peanuts, and catsup. Stir in rice. Spoon mixture into peppers.

2 tablespoons water ¼ cup shredded cheddar cheese (1 ounce)	● Place peppers in an 8x8x2-inch or a 10x6x2-inch baking dish. Add water to dish. Cover dish tightly with foil. Bake in a 350° oven about 35 minutes or till heated through. Uncover and sprinkle with cheese. Bake, uncovered, about 2 minutes more or till cheese melts. Makes 2 servings.

Don't bother to precook the peppers. They'll get crisp-tender while they bake in the oven with the rice filling.

Turkey and Broccoli Rolls

Total Time: 45 minutes

1 **10-ounce package frozen broccoli spears**
2 **cups herb-seasoned stuffing mix**
1 **6-ounce package (6 round slices) sliced turkey luncheon meat**

● Cook broccoli according to package directions; drain. Prepare stuffing mix according to package directions. Spoon stuffing mix into a 10x6x2-inch baking dish. Divide broccoli into 6 portions. Place 1 broccoli portion on each slice of turkey. Roll up.

Place, seam side down, on stuffing in the baking dish (see photo, below).

If turkey's not handy, then ham it up! Sliced boiled ham works just as well.

1 **7¾-ounce can semi-condensed cream of mushroom soup**
⅓ **cup plain yogurt**
½ **teaspoon curry powder**

● In a small mixing bowl stir together soup, yogurt, and curry powder. Pour soup mixture over turkey and stuffing. Cover and bake in a 350° oven for 20 minutes. Uncover and bake about 10 minutes more or till heated through. Makes 3 servings.

Roll each slice of turkey around broccoli. Let some of the broccoli flowerets peek out of the end of each turkey roll. Arrange turkey rolls, seam sides down, on top of stuffing.

Chili-Seasoned Chicken

Preparation: 15 minutes
Cooking Time: 40 minutes

1 large onion, sliced and separated into rings 1 tablespoon cooking oil	● In a heavy 12-inch skillet cook onion in hot oil till tender. With a slotted spoon remove onion and set aside.
1 2½- to 3-pound broiler-fryer chicken, cut up 1 11-ounce can condensed tomato bisque soup ½ cup water 1 1¼-ounce envelope chili seasoning mix	● Brown chicken in remaining oil for 10 minutes, turning once. Drain off fat. Meanwhile, in a small mixing bowl stir together soup, water, and seasoning mix. Return onion to skillet. Pour in soup mixture. Bring to boiling; reduce heat. Cover and simmer for 20 minutes.
1 9-ounce package frozen Italian green beans *or* cut green beans 1 8-ounce can red kidney beans, drained 3 cups hot cooked couscous	● Add green beans and kidney beans to skillet with chicken mixture. Cover and cook for 15 to 20 minutes more or till chicken is tender. Serve chicken mixture with hot cooked couscous. Serves 6.

It's true! All that spicy good flavor comes from just a small envelope of chili seasoning mix.

Couscous is a quick cooker. Simply cover 1 cup ready-to-cook couscous with 1 cup boiling water. Let stand for 3 to 4 minutes and voilà—3 cups hot cooked couscous.

Mac and Cheese Deluxe

Total Time: 25 minutes

1 7¼-ounce package macaroni and cheese dinner mix 1 5-ounce package small smoked sausage links 1 8-ounce package frozen peas in cream sauce	● Cook macaroni dinner mix according to package directions. Meanwhile, cut sausages in half. Set aside. Cook peas according to package directions, *except* omit butter.
½ teaspoon Italian seasoning	● Stir peas, sausages, and seasoning into macaroni and cheese in saucepan. Cook and stir about 5 minutes or till heated through. Makes 4 servings.

Start with a package of macaroni and cheese dinner mix; end up with a hearty, mouth-watering meal in one.

Cooking with 4 Or Fewer Ingredients

When you gather the goods for these recipes, you won't have to look far. We kept the number of ingredients (but not the flavor) to the bare minimum.

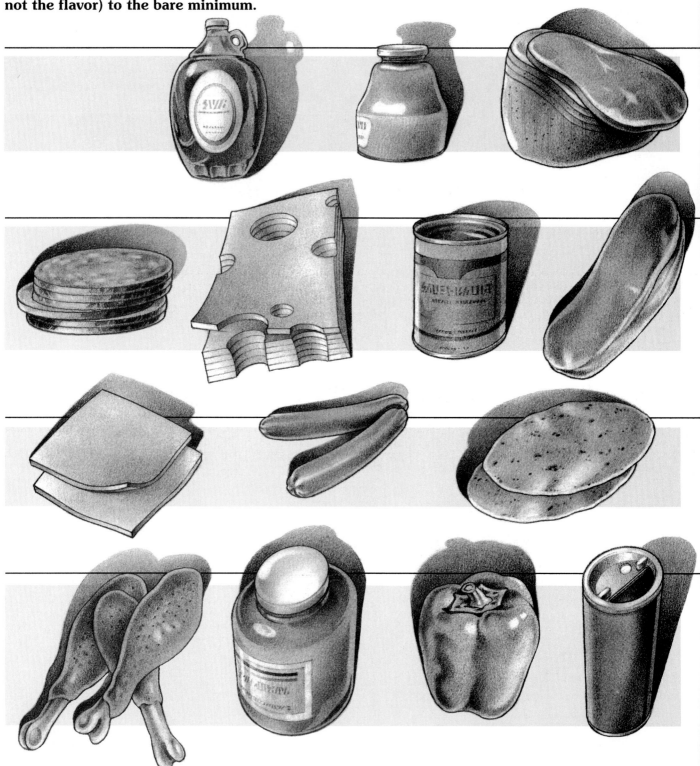

Easy Ham Glaze

Total Time: 10 minutes

¼ cup maple-flavored syrup
2 teaspoons prepared
   mustard
8 ounces sliced fully cooked
   ham, heated

● In a small saucepan combine and heat syrup and mustard. Spoon over ham. Makes 2 servings.

For three hungry people, just increase the meat to 12 ounces and keep the amount of glaze the same. This spunky glaze is also terrific spooned over a baked ham loaf.

Salami Sandwiches

Total Time: 25 minutes

8 slices salami
4 slices Swiss *or* caraway
   cheese
1 8-ounce can sauerkraut,
   rinsed, drained, and
   snipped
4 frankfurter buns, split

● For each sandwich, place *2* slices of salami overlapping each other. Top with *1* slice of cheese. Spoon sauerkraut to within ½ inch of edges. Roll up, from long side, jelly-roll style. Place salami rolls in buns. Wrap in foil. Place on a baking sheet and bake in a 375° oven about 15 minutes or till heated through. Makes 4 servings.

Salami comes in all shapes and sizes. For these sandwiches use round slices that are 4 to 5 inches in diameter.

Chili-Frank Burritos

Total Time: 20 minutes

2 slices American
   cheese (2 ounces)
2 chili-stuffed frankfurters
2 8-inch flour tortillas

● Place *1* slice of cheese and *1* frankfurter on *each* tortilla. Roll up tortillas, folding in sides to form burritos. Wrap in foil. Bake in a 375° oven about 20 minutes or till burritos are heated through. Makes 2 servings.

Uno, dos, tres ingredients for this super south-of-the-border sandwich.

Speedy Cacciatore

Preparation: 15 minutes
Cooking Time: 35 minutes

8 chicken drumsticks *or*
   chicken thighs

● In a medium nonstick skillet cook chicken, skin side down, over medium heat for 15 minutes, turning frequently to brown evenly. Drain off fat.

1 cup spaghetti sauce
1 green pepper, cut into
   ½-inch strips
2 tablespoons grated
   Parmesan cheese

● Add spaghetti sauce and green pepper to skillet. Cover and cook over low heat for 30 to 35 minutes or till chicken is tender. Sprinkle with Parmesan cheese. Makes 4 servings.

For even speedier cacciatore, rely on your microwave oven. Arrange chicken and green pepper in a 12x7½x2-inch nonmetal baking dish. Place the meatiest portions of chicken, skin side down, to the outside. Micro-cook, loosely covered, on 100% power (high) for 10 minutes, turning chicken over and rotating dish once. Drain. Spoon on sauce. Cook 2 to 4 minutes more. Sprinkle with Parmesan.

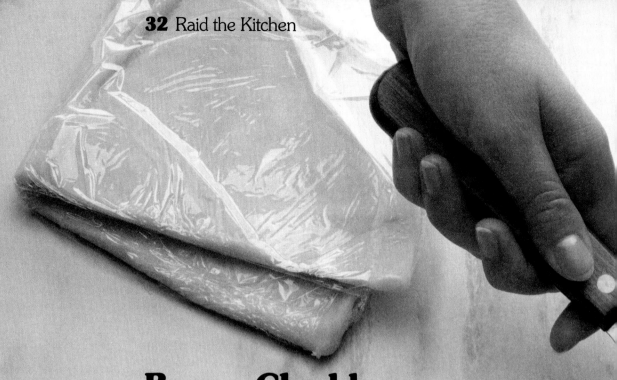

Bacon-Cheddar Quiche

Preparation: 20 minutes
Baking Time: 45 minutes

½ **15-ounce package folded refrigerated unbaked piecrusts (1 crust)**
6 **slices bacon**

● Let piecrust stand at room temperature for 15 to 20 minutes according to package directions. Meanwhile, cook bacon till crisp; drain on paper towels. Crumble bacon.

3 **beaten eggs**
1 **12-ounce can (1½ cups) evaporated milk**
1 **4-ounce package shredded cheddar cheese**
3 **green onions, thinly sliced**

● In a mixing bowl combine eggs and milk. Stir in cheese, onions, and bacon.
    Place piecrust in a 9-inch pie plate. Flute edges high. Line crust with a layer of heavy-duty foil. Bake in a 450° oven for 5 minutes. Carefully remove foil from piecrust and bake about 5 minutes more or till piecrust is nearly done. Remove piecrust from the oven. Reduce the oven temperature to 325°.

● Pour egg mixture into *hot* piecrust. Bake in a 325° oven for 30 to 35 minutes or till a knife inserted near the center comes out clean. Let stand 10 minutes before serving. Makes 6 servings.

This no-measure quiche can be shortcut even more. Simply substitute ¼ cup bacon-flavored vegetable protein chips for the cooked bacon and 1 tablespoon dried minced onion for the sliced green onions.

Saucy Open-Face Sandwiches

Total Time: 20 minutes

12 slices Canadian-style bacon
1 tablespoon butter *or* margarine
1 8-ounce package frozen peas in cream sauce
½ cup shredded cheddar *or* American cheese (2 ounces)

● In a large skillet cook Canadian-style bacon in butter or margarine till light brown. Keep warm.
  Cook frozen peas according to package directions. Stir cheese into hot pea mixture till it melts.

Frozen peas in sauce are the speedy secret to this dinner on the double. Try it for brunch, too.

3 English muffins, split, toasted, and lightly buttered

● Place 2 muffin halves on each of 3 dinner plates. Arrange 2 slices of bacon on each muffin half. Spoon pea mixture over bacon. Makes 3 servings.

Triple-Cheese Pizza

Total Time: 35 minutes

1 cup frozen chopped broccoli
½ cup cream-style cottage cheese
1 egg
2 tablespoons grated Parmesan cheese
¼ teaspoon dried basil, crushed

● Cook broccoli according to package directions; drain. Cut up any large pieces.
  Meanwhile, in a blender container or food processor bowl combine cottage cheese and egg. Cover and blend till smooth. Stir in broccoli, Parmesan cheese, and basil.

Bring home a frozen cheese pizza and . . . ta-da! It quickly becomes a magnificent meatless meal for four.

1 11-ounce frozen cheese pizza
¾ cup shredded mozzarella *or* cheddar cheese (3 ounces)

● Place pizza on a greased baking sheet. Spread broccoli mixture over frozen pizza to within 1 inch of the edges. Sprinkle with mozzarella or cheddar cheese. Bake in a 400° oven for 20 to 25 minutes or till heated through. Makes 4 servings.

Crustless Quiche

**Preparation: 15 minutes
Baking Time: 35 minutes**

1 10-ounce package frozen
  chopped spinach
2 cups shredded cheddar
  cheese (8 ounces)

● Cook spinach according to package directions; drain well. Press spinach evenly into the bottom of a greased 10-inch pie plate or quiche dish. Sprinkle with cheddar cheese.

1½ cups milk
 1 8½-ounce package corn
   muffin mix
 4 eggs
 ¼ teaspoon onion powder
 ¼ cup grated Parmesan
   cheese

● In a mixing bowl combine milk, muffin mix, eggs, and onion powder. Beat with a rotary beater till well combined. Pour over spinach mixture in pie plate. Sprinkle with Parmesan.
  Bake in a 350° oven about 35 minutes or till top is brown and springs back when lightly touched. Let stand 5 minutes before serving. Makes 6 servings.

We call this tasty dish "crustless quiche," but it's really a cross between a quiche and spoon bread. No matter what you call it, it's a breeze to make and a pleasure to eat.

Microwave Cooking Tips

Busy schedules and microwave cooking go hand in hand. Shortcut your time in the kitchen with these tips:
● Don't wait around for butter or margarine to soften. Unwrap it and place it in a small nonmetal dish. Micro-cook on 10% power (low) about 30 seconds for 2 tablespoons or 50 to 60 seconds for ¼ cup.
● Soften a 3-ounce package of cream cheese by unwrapping it and placing it in a small nonmetal bowl. Micro-cook, uncovered, on 30% power (medium-low) about 1 minute.
● No need to throw out stale chips, pretzels, or crackers. Crisp them in your microwave oven. Spread one cup of the stale snack in a shallow nonmetal baking dish. Micro-cook, uncovered, on 100% power (high) for 30 to 45 seconds. Let stand 1 minute.
● Because all microwave ovens do not have the same power, check the wattage listed on the oven and in the owner's manual. We tested our recipes in 600- to 700-watt ovens. If your microwave oven differs, use your owner's manual as a guide for cooking times.

Busy People's Beef Stew

Total Time: 20 minutes

---

1 8-ounce can red kidney
   beans, drained
1 7½-ounce can beef stew
1 6-ounce can vegetable
   juice cocktail
1 cup loose-pack frozen
   mixed broccoli, corn,
   and peppers
1 2½-ounce jar sliced
   mushrooms, drained
¼ cup shredded cheddar *or*
   Swiss cheese (1 ounce)

● In a medium saucepan combine beans, beef stew, vegetable juice, frozen vegetables, and mushrooms.

Cook, uncovered, over medium heat about 15 minutes or till vegetables are crisp-tender, stirring occasionally. Sprinkle with cheese. Makes 2 servings.

A fantastic fix-up of canned beef stew. For extra pizzazz, use hot-style vegetable juice cocktail.

Microwave Method: In a 1-quart nonmetal casserole combine beans, beef stew, vegetable juice, frozen vegetables, and mushrooms. Micro-cook, covered, on 100% power (high) for 7 to 8 minutes or till vegetables are crisp-tender, stirring twice. Sprinkle with cheese.

Mini Mock Lasagna

Total Time: 35 minutes

1 15-ounce can cheese *or* beef ravioli in sauce, *or* cheese ravioli and meatballs

● Spoon *half* of the ravioli into 2 individual baking dishes.

When you don't want to heat up the oven, use a toaster oven to bake this easy-on-the-cook lasagna.

1 beaten egg yolk
½ cup cream-style cottage cheese
2 tablespoons grated Parmesan cheese
⅛ teaspoon dried oregano, crushed
Dash garlic powder

● In a mixing bowl stir together egg yolk, cottage cheese, Parmesan cheese, oregano, and garlic powder. Spoon over ravioli in baking dishes. Spoon remaining ravioli over cottage cheese mixture.

½ cup shredded mozzarella cheese (2 ounces)

● Sprinkle mozzarella cheese over ravioli in baking dishes. Bake in a 375° oven for 20 to 25 minutes or till heated through. Makes 2 servings.

Microwave Method: Spoon *half* of the ravioli into 2 individual microwave-safe baking dishes. In a mixing bowl stir together egg yolk, cottage cheese, Parmesan cheese, oregano, and garlic powder. Spoon over ravioli in baking dishes. Spoon remaining ravioli over cottage cheese mixture.

Micro-cook, covered, on 100% power (high) for 6 to 7 minutes or till heated through. Uncover. Sprinkle with mozzarella cheese. Cook about 30 seconds more or till cheese melts.

Hot Tuna Sandwich Cups

Preparation: 25 minutes
Baking Time: 20 minutes

1 **package (6) refrigerated biscuits**
2 **6½-ounce cans tuna (water pack), drained and flaked**
½ **cup shredded cheddar cheese (2 ounces)**
1 **medium green onion, sliced**
¼ **cup creamy buttermilk salad dressing**
2 **tablespoons sweet pickle relish**

● Separate biscuit dough into 6 biscuits. Grease the *outside* of six 6-ounce custard cups. Press 1 portion of dough around the outside of each custard cup, covering the bottom of the cup and halfway down the sides.

Place cups, dough side up, on an ungreased 15x10x1-inch baking pan. Bake in a 400° oven about 7 minutes or till light brown.

Meanwhile, in a medium mixing bowl stir together tuna, cheese, onion, salad dressing, and pickle relish.

1. Press one biscuit around the outside of each greased custard cup.

● When biscuits are done, immediately remove them from custard cups and place on a wire rack. Spoon about ⅓ cup tuna mixture into each cup.

3 **thin tomato slices**
¼ **cup shredded cheddar cheese (1 ounce)**
Celery leaves (optional)

● Place *half* of the filled cups on a 15x10x1-inch baking pan. Bake in a 400° oven about 7 minutes or till filling is heated through. Freeze the remaining cups according to directions below. Place tomato slices on hot tuna filling. Sprinkle with cheese. Bake for 2 to 3 minutes more or till cheese melts. Garnish with celery leaves, if desired. Makes 6 servings, total (3 frozen).

Reheating Time: 65 minutes

● **To freeze tuna cups,** wrap remaining filled cups in heavy-duty foil. Seal, label, and freeze up to 6 months.

To reheat the frozen tuna cups, place the frozen foil-wrapped cups on a 15x10x1-inch baking pan. Bake in a 350° oven for 55 to 60 minutes or till heated through. Unwrap. Place 3 thin *tomato slices* on hot tuna filling. Sprinkle with ¼ cup shredded *cheddar cheese.* Bake for 2 to 3 minutes more or till cheese melts. Garnish with *celery leaves,* if desired.

2. Remove baked biscuits from custard cups. Place on a wire rack.

3. Spoon tuna mixture into biscuit cups.

4. Top with tomato slices. Sprinkle with cheese. Bake for 2 to 3 minutes more or till cheese melts.

Pastry-Topped Salmon Patties

Total Time: 40 minutes

1 10-ounce package (6)
    frozen patty shells
1 beaten egg
⅓ cup milk
1½ cups soft whole wheat
    bread crumbs (2 slices)
3 medium carrots, shredded
2 stalks celery, finely
    chopped
2 medium green onions,
    finely chopped
1 teaspoon prepared
    horseradish
1 teaspoon soy sauce
¼ teaspoon pepper
1 15½-ounce can salmon,
    drained, flaked, and
    skin and bones removed

● Remove package of patty shells from the freezer to thaw (or thaw overnight in the refrigerator).

Meanwhile, in a mixing bowl combine egg and milk. Stir in crumbs, carrots, celery, onions, horseradish, soy sauce, and pepper. Add salmon. Mix well.

Shape into 6 patties about 3½ inches in diameter. Place *half* of the patties on a greased baking sheet. Place the remaining salmon patties on another greased baking sheet.

On a lightly floured surface roll each patty shell into a 6-inch circle.

Milk
Dairy sour cream *or*
    plain yogurt (optional)

● On a lightly floured surface roll each patty shell into a 6-inch circle. Drape each pastry circle over a salmon patty (see photos, right). Flute edges. Brush with milk. Freeze *half* of the patties according to directions below.

Bake remaining patties, uncovered, in a 425° oven for 15 to 20 minutes or till pastry is golden brown. Serve warm. Top with sour cream or yogurt, if desired. Makes 6 servings, total (3 frozen).

Drape each pastry circle over a salmon patty. For a decorative look, flute the edges of the pastry.

**Reheating Time:
45 minutes**

● **To freeze patties,** place remaining patties on baking sheet in the freezer about 1 hour or till patties are firm. Remove patties from baking sheet. Transfer to a freezer container or moisture- and vaporproof wrap. Seal, label, and freeze up to 6 months.

To bake, place frozen patties on a greased baking sheet. Bake, uncovered, in a 350° oven for 40 to 45 minutes or till patties are heated through and pastry is golden brown. Serve warm.

Chunky Spaghetti Sauce

Preparation: 30 minutes
Cooking Time: 30 minutes

1 pound ground beef
1 medium onion, chopped
1 stalk celery, chopped
1 small green pepper, chopped
2 cloves garlic, minced

● For the meat sauce, in a Dutch oven cook meat, onion, celery, green pepper, and garlic till meat is brown and onion is tender. Drain off fat.

Dare to be different. Serve this chunky sauce over hot cooked corkscrew pasta instead of spaghetti.

2 16-ounce cans tomatoes, cut up
2 4-ounce cans sliced mushrooms
1 6-ounce can tomato paste
½ cup sliced pitted ripe olives
¼ cup water
2 teaspoons sugar
1 teaspoon dried basil, crushed
½ teaspoon salt
½ teaspoon dried thyme, crushed
½ teaspoon dried oregano, crushed
1 bay leaf

● Stir in *undrained* tomatoes, *undrained* mushrooms, tomato paste, olives, water, sugar, basil, salt, thyme, oregano, and bay leaf. Bring to boiling; reduce heat. Simmer, uncovered, about 30 minutes or to desired consistency, stirring occasionally. Remove the bay leaf.

8 ounces spaghetti, cooked and drained
Fresh basil (optional)

● Serve *half* of the sauce over cooked spaghetti. Garnish with basil, if desired. Freeze remaining according to directions below. Makes 8 servings, total (4 frozen).

Reheating Time:
45 minutes

● **To freeze the sauce,** pour the remaining sauce into a 4-cup freezer container. Seal, label, and freeze the mixture up to 6 months.
   To reheat the sauce, place frozen sauce and 2 tablespoons *water* into a medium saucepan. Cover and cook over medium-low heat for 40 to 45 minutes or till heated through, stirring occasionally. Serve with 8 ounces *spaghetti,* cooked and drained.

Gingered Lamb Stir-Fry

Preparation: 30 minutes
Cooking Time: 20 minutes

1 **pound boneless lamb** 3 **tablespoons soy sauce** 2 **tablespoons cornstarch** ¼ **teaspoon instant chicken** **bouillon granules**	● If desired, partially freeze meat. Thinly slice across the grain into bite-size strips. For sauce, stir together soy sauce, cornstarch, and instant chicken bouillon granules. Set aside.

1 **tablespoon cooking oil**
2 **teaspoons grated**
   gingerroot
1 **clove garlic, minced**
8 **green onions, bias-sliced**
   into 1-inch pieces
3 **medium carrots, thinly**
   bias sliced
	● Preheat a wok or large skillet over high heat. Add oil. (Add more oil as necessary during cooking.) Stir-fry gingerroot and garlic in hot oil for 15 seconds. Add onions. Stir-fry for 1½ to 2 minutes or till onions are tender. Remove onion mixture from wok. Add carrots to wok. Stir-fry for 4 to 5 minutes or till crisp-tender. Remove from wok.

	● Add *half* of the lamb to the hot wok. Stir-fry about 3 minutes or till just tender. Remove from wok. Stir-fry remaining lamb about 3 minutes or till just tender. Return all meat to wok. Push meat from center of wok.
1⅓ **cups water** 1 **cup hot cooked rice**	● Stir sauce. Add to center of wok along with water. Cook and stir till thickened and bubbly. Cook and stir 2 minutes more. Stir in carrot and onion mixture. Heat through. Serve *half* of the lamb mixture with rice. Freeze remaining lamb mixture according to directions below. Makes 4 servings, total (2 frozen).

Reheating Time:
   20 minutes
	● **To freeze lamb mixture,** spoon remaining lamb mixture into a 1½- to 2-cup freezer container. Seal, label, and freeze up to 6 months.
	   To reheat, place frozen mixture in a small saucepan. Add 1 tablespoon *water.* Cover and cook over medium-low heat for 15 to 20 minutes or till heated through, stirring occasionally. Serve with 1 cup *hot cooked rice.*

It is said that the old kings of the Orient ate gingerroot boiled in honey. We simply grate the gingerroot for this fabulous stir-fry.

When buying gingerroot, squeeze the knobby root to make sure it's solid and firm. When you cut into the gingerroot, the flesh should be very aromatic and pale yellow. Avoid using gingerroot with dark areas on its flesh.

Spicy Turkey Chili

Total Time: 45 minutes

Put your boxing gloves on; this chili packs a punch!

1 pound ground raw turkey
1 medium onion, chopped
3 cloves garlic, minced

● In a Dutch oven cook turkey, onion, and garlic till meat is brown and onion is tender. Drain off fat.

2 28-ounce cans tomatoes, cut up
1 15½-ounce can red kidney beans, drained
1 12-ounce can beer
1 4-ounce can diced green chili peppers, drained
1 tablespoon chili powder
2 teaspoons Italian seasoning
1 teaspoon sugar
1 teaspoon ground cumin
1 teaspoon bottled hot pepper sauce
½ teaspoon ground allspice
½ cup shredded cheddar cheese (2 ounces)

● Stir in *undrained* tomatoes, kidney beans, beer, green chili peppers, chili powder, Italian seasoning, sugar, cumin, hot pepper sauce, allspice, and ½ teaspoon *pepper*. Bring to boiling; reduce heat. Simmer, uncovered, for 30 minutes or to desired consistency.

Spoon *half* of the mixture into serving bowls. Sprinkle with cheese. Freeze remaining according to directions below. Makes 8 servings, total (4 frozen).

Reheating Time: 50 minutes

● **To freeze the chili,** spoon the remaining chili into a 2-quart freezer container. Seal, label, and freeze up to 6 months.

To reheat chili, transfer frozen mixture to a large saucepan. Cover and cook over medium-low heat about 50 minutes or till heated through, stirring occasionally. Spoon into bowls. Sprinkle with ½ cup shredded *cheddar cheese*.

Foolproof Freezing

Freezing foods is a great way for busy families to enjoy no-fuss meals. Here's a quick checklist to ensure that what you take out of the freezer is just as good as it was when you put it in.

● Set your freezer temperature at 0° F or below to maintain the best food color, flavor, and texture.

● Quickly cool hot foods before freezing.

● Use moisture- and vaporproof wrap and containers that are recommended for freezing.

● Label and date each package you freeze.

● Separate packages in the freezer till they're solidly frozen. This allows cold air to circulate around them.

● Limit how much food you freeze at one time. Freeze only two to three pounds of food per cubic foot of total storage space within a 24-hour period.

Double-Up Zucchini Lasagna

Preparation: 45 minutes
Baking Time: 45 minutes

---

1 medium onion, chopped
2 cloves garlic, minced
1 tablespoon butter *or* margarine
1 16-ounce can tomatoes, cut up
1 medium zucchini, shredded (1¼ cups)
1 8-ounce can pizza sauce
1 6-ounce can tomato paste
2 teaspoons dried basil, crushed

● In a large skillet cook onion and garlic in butter or margarine till onion is tender. Stir in *undrained* tomatoes, zucchini, pizza sauce, tomato paste, and basil. Bring to boiling; reduce heat. Cover and simmer for 15 minutes, stirring often.

Thank goodness you can keep an extra batch of this vegetarian lasagna on hand in the freezer. It's sure to be a favorite.

---

8 lasagna noodles
2 beaten eggs
2 cups ricotta cheese
½ cup grated Parmesan cheese
2 tablespoons snipped parsley
½ teaspoon pepper

● Meanwhile, cook noodles according to package directions; drain. Rinse with cold water. Drain.
In a medium mixing bowl stir together eggs, ricotta cheese, Parmesan cheese, parsley, and pepper.

---

2 6-ounce packages sliced mozzarella cheese
¼ cup grated Parmesan cheese

● To assemble, place *2* noodles in *each* of *two* 10x6x2-inch baking dishes, trimming to fit. Spread *each* dish with *one-fourth* of the ricotta cheese mixture. Top *each* with *one-fourth* of the mozzarella cheese and *one-fourth* of the zucchini mixture. Repeat layers once. Sprinkle *each* with *half* of the Parmesan.
Cover 1 of the baking dishes with foil. Bake in a 375° oven for 40 to 45 minutes or till heated through. Let stand 10 minutes before serving. Freeze remaining dish according to directions below. Makes 8 servings, total (4 frozen).

Reheating Time:
1½ hours

● **To freeze lasagna,** seal the remaining baking dish with moisture- and vaporproof wrap, label, and freeze up to 6 months.
To bake lasagna, place frozen lasagna in baking dish in a 375° oven. Bake, covered, about 1½ hours or till hot. Let stand 10 minutes before serving.

Individual Shrimp Stratas

Preparation: 20 minutes
Baking Time: 25 minutes

1 **6-ounce package frozen cooked shrimp**
1½ **cups croutons**

● Place shrimp in a colander. Run cool water over shrimp for 1 minute. Drain. Pat shrimp dry with paper towels. Place croutons in 4 au gratin dishes or four 14- to 16-ounce shallow individual casseroles. Top with shrimp.

1 **7½-ounce can semi-condensed cream of mushroom soup**
3 **eggs**
1 **cup shredded cheddar cheese (4 ounces)**
⅓ **cup milk**
¼ **teaspoon finely shredded lemon peel**
⅛ **teaspoon dried tarragon, crushed**
3 **medium green onions, sliced**

● In a blender container or food processor bowl place soup, eggs, cheese, milk, lemon peel, and tarragon. Cover and blend till smooth. Stir in onion. Pour over shrimp mixture in au gratin dishes. Cover and refrigerate at least 1 hour or up to 24 hours.

1 **10-ounce package frozen asparagus spears** *or* **broccoli spears**

● Bake shrimp mixture, uncovered, in a 350° oven about 25 minutes or till a knife inserted near the center comes out clean. Let stand for 5 minutes.

Meanwhile, cook vegetables according to package directions. Drain well. Arrange cooked vegetables on top of shrimp mixture. Makes 4 servings.

Perfect for the family with different eating schedules. Whether you're busy with a meeting, a ball game, or a shopping expedition— these stratas are ready when you are.

Tuna-Vermicelli Salad

Preparation: 35 minutes

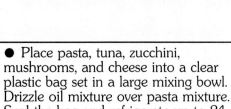

3 ounces vermicelli, broken
  into 2- to 3-inch pieces
⅓ cup salad oil
⅓ cup white wine vinegar
1 teaspoon dried basil,
  crushed
¼ teaspoon salt
¼ teaspoon garlic powder
⅛ teaspoon pepper

● Cook pasta according to package directions; drain. Rinse. Drain again.

In a screw-top jar combine oil, vinegar, basil, salt, garlic powder, and pepper. Cover and shake well.

Place the pasta mixture into a clear plastic bag set in a mixing bowl. Be sure to use a heavy plastic bag with a good seal. Add salad dressing. Seal bag and refrigerate up to 24 hours, turning the plastic bag occasionally to distribute marinade.

1 9¼-ounce can tuna (water
  pack), drained
1 small zucchini, cut into
  julienne strips
1 cup sliced fresh
  mushrooms
½ cup cubed cheddar cheese
  (2 ounces)
2 medium tomatoes,
  chopped
  Grated Parmesan cheese
  (optional)

● Place pasta, tuna, zucchini, mushrooms, and cheese into a clear plastic bag set in a large mixing bowl. Drizzle oil mixture over pasta mixture. Seal the bag and refrigerate up to 24 hours, turning bag occasionally.

Before serving, remove pasta mixture from plastic bag. Toss with tomatoes. Sprinkle with Parmesan cheese, if desired. Serves 4.

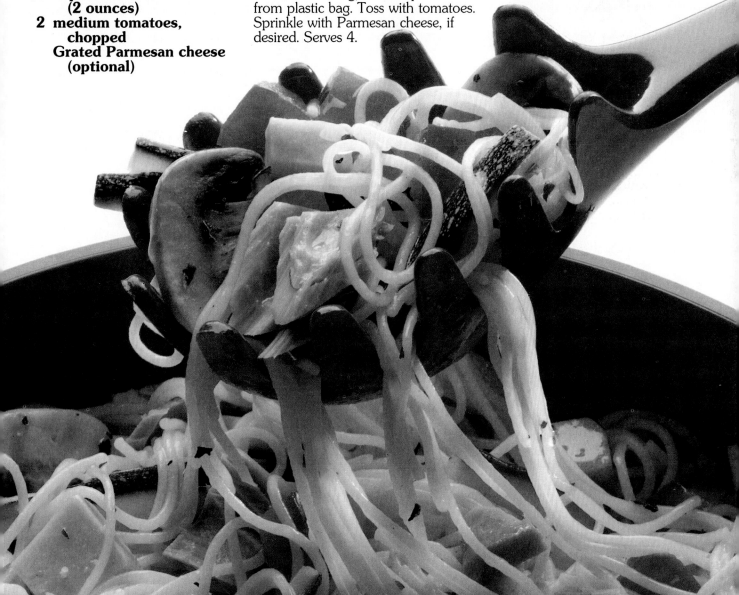

Sweet 'n' Sour Beef Kabobs

Preparation: 20 minutes
Cooking Time: 10 minutes

1   8¼-ounce can pineapple chunks
1   pound beef sirloin steak, cut into 1-inch cubes
1   medium green pepper, cut into 1-inch squares, *or* 2 small onions, cut into wedges
⅓   cup catsup
2   tablespoons vinegar
1   teaspoon instant beef bouillon granules
¼   teaspoon ground cinnamon
⅛   teaspoon ground allspice

● Drain pineapple, reserving liquid. Add water to liquid to measure ½ cup total liquid. Place meat cubes and green pepper or onions in a plastic bag. Set bag in a bowl. Cover and refrigerate the pineapple chunks.

For marinade, combine pineapple liquid, catsup, vinegar, bouillon granules, cinnamon, and allspice. Pour over beef cubes in bag. Close bag.

Marinate meat and vegetables in the refrigerator up to 24 hours, turning the bag several times.

Make the most of the extra marinade. Heat it in a heatproof bowl right on the grill with the kabobs. Then spoon it over the meat and rice.

Hot cooked rice

● Drain meat, reserving marinade. On 4 skewers alternately thread meat, green pepper squares or onion wedges, and pineapple. Grill kabobs, on an uncovered grill, over *medium-hot* coals to desired doneness, allowing 9 to 11 minutes for medium. Turn and brush often with reserved marinade during grilling. Serve kabobs with rice. Pass remaining marinade. Makes 4 servings.

Teriyaki Lamb Chops

Preparation: 10 minutes
Cooking Time: 10 minutes

2   lamb leg sirloin chops, cut ¾ inch thick (8 to 10 ounces total)
1   tablespoon dry white wine
1   tablespoon soy sauce
1½ teaspoons cooking oil
¼   teaspoon ground ginger

● Trim chops of separable fat. Place in a pie plate. For marinade, in a small mixing bowl stir together wine, soy sauce, oil, and ginger. Pour over meat.

We rated these with a triple T (terrific teriyaki taste), thanks to a blend of wine, soy sauce, and ground ginger.

● Cover and marinate the chops at room temperature for 1 hour or in the refrigerator up to 24 hours, turning occasionally. Drain chops, reserving the marinade.

● Broil chops 3 to 4 inches from the heat for 4 minutes. Turn and broil to desired doneness, allowing 4 minutes more for medium. Brush frequently with marinade during broiling. Serves 2.

Sausage-Spud Kabobs

Preparation: 15 minutes
Cooking Time: 20 minutes

2 cups water
1 tablespoon pickling spice
½ teaspoon onion salt
3 medium carrots, cut into
  1-inch pieces
2 medium red potatoes,
  quartered

● In a large saucepan combine the water, pickling spice, and onion salt. Bring to boiling. Add the carrots. Reduce heat. Cover and simmer for 10 minutes. Remove from heat. Meanwhile, cook potatoes in boiling water about 10 minutes or till tender. Drain. Cover and chill potatoes.

Hold those spuds! Don't marinate the cooked potatoes with the sausage and carrots. The potatoes tone down the piquant flavor of the marinated ingredients.

½ cup vinegar
⅓ cup sugar
1 pound fully cooked
  Polish sausage

● Add vinegar and sugar to hot carrot mixture. Cut the Polish sausage into 1½-inch pieces. Cut 1 or 2 slashes into each piece, about ¼ inch deep. Add to the carrot mixture. Cover and marinate at room temperature for 20 minutes or in the refrigerator up to 24 hours. Stir mixture occasionally.

Melted butter *or*
  margarine (optional)

● Drain vegetable-sausage mixture. Thread potatoes, carrots, and Polish sausage alternately on skewers. Place on the rack of an unheated broiler pan. Broil 4 inches from the heat for 7 to 9 minutes or till heated through, turning once. Brush potatoes with melted butter or margarine, if desired. Serves 4.

Make Now, Serve Later

You're a busy person. So get the most out of every minute you spend in the kitchen by making food ahead. With the recipes in this chapter, you can make delicious meals 24 hours in advance. Simply prepare the food one night, pop it in the refrigerator, and enjoy it hassle-free the next night.

To help you easily slot these recipes into your schedule, we've given the preparation time for each recipe. For those that require cooking after being chilled, we've listed that time, too.

Mexican Make-Ahead Menu

Olé! Treat your family to the tantalizing flavors of Mexico. It's mucho simple when you make most of it the night before. At dinnertime, set out a chilled pitcher of sangria for adults or fruit juice for kids.

Chorizo-Tortilla Casserole
(see recipe, page 52)

MENU
Chorizo-Tortilla Casserole
Cool 'n' Creamy Avocado Soup
Jicama-Corn Salad

MENU COUNTDOWN
The Night Before
Assemble Chorizo-Tortilla Casserole, Cool 'n' Creamy Avocado Soup, and vegetable mixture for Jicama-Corn Salad. Cover and chill.
1 Hour Ahead
Bake casserole. Tear lettuce for salad.
5 Minutes Ahead
Spoon soup into bowls. If desired, top with sliced avocado and sprinkle with sunflower nuts. Spoon salad onto lettuce.

Cool 'n' Creamy Avocado Soup
(see recipe, page 53)

Jicama-Corn Salad
(see recipe, page 53)

Chorizo-Tortilla Casserole

Preparation: 20 minutes
Baking Time: 55 minutes

Pictured on pages 50–51.

½ pound bulk chorizo *or*
    Italian sausage
1 medium onion, chopped
5 6-inch corn tortillas

● In a medium saucepan cook meat and onion till meat is brown and onion is tender. Drain off fat. Meanwhile, cut tortillas into strips about 3 inches long and ½ inch wide.

Chorizo (chuh REE zoh) is a highly spiced sausage that's popular in Mexican cooking. Look for it at ethnic markets.

1 10-ounce can tomatoes
    and green chili peppers
1 6-ounce can tomato juice
½ teaspoon sugar
½ teaspoon dried oregano,
    crushed
¼ teaspoon pepper

● Stir tomatoes and chili peppers, juice, sugar, oregano, and pepper into meat mixture. Bring to boiling; reduce heat. Cover. Simmer for 5 minutes; remove from heat. Stir in tortilla strips.

¼ cup shredded cheddar *or*
    Monterey Jack cheese
    (1 ounce)
  Fresh cilantro *or* parsley
    sprigs (optional)

● Spoon meat mixture into a 1-quart casserole. Cover and refrigerate up to 24 hours.
    Cover and bake in a 350° oven about 50 minutes or till heated through. Sprinkle with cheese. Bake, uncovered, for 2 to 3 minutes more or till cheese melts. Garnish with fresh cilantro or parsley, if desired. Makes 4 servings.

Microwave Method: In a 1-quart nonmetal casserole micro-cook meat and onion, uncovered, on 100% power (high) for 3 to 5 minutes or till meat is brown and onion is tender, stirring once to break up meat. Drain off fat. Meanwhile, cut tortillas into strips 3 inches long and ½ inch wide.
    Stir tomatoes and green chili peppers, tomato juice, sugar, oregano, and pepper into meat mixture. Cook, covered, on high about 5 minutes or till bubbly, stirring once. Stir in tortillas. Cover and refrigerate several hours or overnight.
    Cook, covered, on 70% power (medium-high) for 10 to 15 minutes or till heated through, stirring once. Sprinkle with cheese. Cook on high about 1 minute or till cheese melts. Garnish with fresh cilantro or parsley, if desired.

Jicama-Corn Salad

Preparation: 15 minutes

Pictured on pages 50–51.

1 8¾-ounce can whole kernel corn, drained 6 ounces jicama, peeled and cut into ½-inch cubes (1 cup), *or* one 8-ounce can sliced water chestnuts, drained 1 green onion, sliced 2 tablespoons sliced pitted ripe olives 1 tablespoon chopped pimiento	● In a medium mixing bowl combine corn, jicama or water chestnuts, onion, olives, and pimiento.
3 tablespoons salad oil 2 tablespoons white wine vinegar ½ teaspoon sugar ¼ teaspoon garlic powder	● For dressing, in a screw-top jar combine oil, vinegar, sugar, and garlic powder. Cover and shake well. Pour over corn mixture in bowl, stirring to coat. Cover and refrigerate up to 24 hours, stirring occasionally.
Torn lettuce	● To serve, spoon corn mixture onto lettuce with a slotted spoon. Serves 4.

Jicama (HEE kuh muh) is known as the Mexican version of a water chestnut, and it's no wonder. Both jicama and water chestnuts have the same delightful crunch. You can substitute one for the other in most recipes.

Cool 'n' Creamy Avocado Soup

Preparation: 15 minutes

Pictured on pages 50–51.

1 8-ounce carton dairy sour cream 1 cup loosely packed fresh basil, oregano, *or* parsley 1 medium avocado, peeled, pitted, and cut up ½ cup milk 2 small *or* 1 large green onion, sliced 1 tablespoon lemon juice	● In a blender container or food processor bowl combine sour cream; basil, oregano, or parsley; avocado; milk; onion; and lemon juice. Cover and blend till smooth.
1 cup chicken broth	● Pour mixture into a 4-cup container. Stir in chicken broth. Completely cover surface of avocado mixture with clear plastic wrap. Seal the container and refrigerate up to 24 hours.
Avocado slices (optional) Sunflower nuts (optional)	● To serve, remove plastic wrap. Stir. Spoon chilled mixture into soup bowls. Float an avocado slice in each bowl and sprinkle with sunflower nuts, if desired. Makes 4 servings.

This cold refreshing soup tempers the spicy chorizo casserole.

When making the soup ahead, be sure to cover its surface with plastic wrap. This prevents the avocado in the soup from turning brown. Or, if you like, omit the avocado initially. Then blend it with the soup just before serving.

Pork Chop Suey

Preparation: 30 minutes
Cooking Time: 10½ hours

Oriental cooking in a crockery cooker! After work, just make the rice and get out the chopsticks.

1 **pound lean boneless pork** *or* **beef** 1 **tablespoon cooking oil**	● Cut meat into ¾-inch cubes. In a large skillet cook pork or beef, half at a time, in hot oil till brown. Drain off fat.
2 **stalks celery, sliced** 2 **medium carrots, cut into** ¼**-inch slices** 1 **medium red** *or* **green sweet pepper, cut into 1-inch pieces** 1 **medium onion, sliced and separated into rings** 1⅓ **cups beef broth** ¼ **teaspoon ground ginger** ⅛ **teaspoon garlic powder**	● Place meat, celery, carrots, green pepper, and onion in an electric crockery cooker. Stir together broth, ginger, and garlic powder. Pour over meat and vegetable mixture in cooker.
3 **tablespoons soy sauce** 2 **tablespoons cornstarch** 2 **cups fresh bean sprouts** *or* **one 16-ounce can bean sprouts, drained** 1 **4-ounce can sliced mushrooms, drained**	● Cover and cook on low-heat setting for 8 to 10 hours. Turn to high-heat setting. Stir together soy sauce and cornstarch. Stir into pork mixture. Stir in bean sprouts and mushrooms. Cover and cook about 30 minutes more or till thickened and bubbly.
Hot cooked rice ½ **cup chopped peanuts** *or* **cashews**	● Serve over rice. Sprinkle with chopped nuts. Makes 4 servings.

Tarragon Chicken with Squash and Apple Rings

Preparation: 15 minutes
Baking Time: 50 minutes

1 **medium acorn squash (about 1 pound)**
2 **large cooking apples, cored**
2 **whole medium chicken breasts, halved lengthwise**
   Salt
   Pepper

● Cut squash crosswise into 1-inch-thick slices. Discard seeds. Slice each apple into 4 rings.

In a 13x9x2-inch baking dish arrange chicken breasts in a row down half of the dish. Alternate and overlap squash and apple rings down the other half of the dish (see photo, below). Sprinkle lightly with salt and pepper.

The apple of your eye for this dish should be Rome Beauty, York Imperial, Newtown Pippin, Gravenstein, Granny Smith, or Golden Delicious.

¼ **cup butter or margarine, melted**
2 **tablespoons lemon juice**
1½ **teaspoons dried tarragon, crushed**
1 **teaspoon paprika**

● Stir together butter or margarine, lemon juice, tarragon, and paprika. Brush over chicken, squash, and apples. Cover and bake in a 350° oven about 50 minutes or till chicken is done and squash and apples are tender. Transfer to a serving platter with a slotted spoon. Makes 4 servings.

Arrange the chicken breasts in a lengthwise row down half of the baking dish. Alternate and overlap the squash and apple rings down the other half of the dish. Red cooking apples are particularly attractive with the squash.

Orange Chicken

Preparation: 20 minutes
Cooking Time: 6½ hours

4 chicken drumsticks and 4 chicken thighs, skinned (2 pounds total)
2 small green *or* sweet red peppers, cut into strips
½ cup chicken broth
½ cup orange juice
½ cup catsup
2 tablespoons soy sauce
1 tablespoon molasses
1 teaspoon dry mustard
¼ teaspoon garlic powder

1 11-ounce can mandarin orange sections
2 teaspoons cornstarch
¼ cup sliced pitted ripe olives
Hot cooked rice

● Arrange chicken in the bottom of an electric crockery cooker. Top with green or red pepper. In a medium mixing bowl stir together chicken broth, orange juice, catsup, soy sauce, molasses, dry mustard, garlic powder, and ⅛ teaspoon *pepper*. Pour over chicken in crockery cooker. Cover and cook on low-heat setting about 6 hours or till chicken is tender.

Remove chicken and peppers from cooker. Keep warm. Reserve drippings.

● For sauce, skim fat from drippings. Measure *1 cup* cooking liquid. Transfer to a saucepan. Drain oranges, reserving *1 tablespoon* juice. Stir together reserved juice and cornstarch. Add to liquid in saucepan. Cook and stir till thickened and bubbly. Cook and stir 2 minutes more. Stir in oranges and olives. Heat through. Serve sauce and chicken mixture over rice. Makes 4 servings.

This 6-hour crockery-cooked meal is ideal for starting during your lunch hour.

You also can wait till after work and prepare this dish in the oven. Simply follow the recipe as directed, *except* arrange the crockery cooker ingredients in a 2- or 3-quart casserole. Cover and bake in a 350° oven for 1 hour or till chicken is tender.

Lazy Day Chicken Lasagna

Preparation: 15 minutes
Baking Time: 60 minutes

1 cup spaghetti sauce with mushrooms
1 cup frozen diced cooked chicken
½ teaspoon dried basil, crushed
1 beaten egg
¾ cup cream-style cottage cheese, drained
¼ cup grated Parmesan cheese
1 tablespoon dried parsley flakes
4 lasagna noodles
1 cup shredded mozzarella cheese (4 ounces)

⅓ cup boiling water

● In a mixing bowl combine spaghetti sauce, chicken, and basil. Set aside. In a mixing bowl stir together beaten egg, cottage cheese, Parmesan cheese, parsley flakes, and ⅛ teaspoon *pepper*.

Place 2 of the *uncooked* lasagna noodles in a 10x6x2-inch baking dish. Layer with *half* of the chicken mixture, *half* of the cottage cheese mixture, and *half* of the shredded mozzarella cheese. Repeat the layers, *except* for the remaining mozzarella cheese.

● Pour boiling water into the dish around the edges. Cover tightly with foil. Bake in a 350° oven about 60 minutes or till noodles are tender. Sprinkle with remaining mozzarella cheese. Let stand, covered, for 10 minutes. Serves 4.

The timesaving trick here is to assemble the lasagna using uncooked noodles.

To test the noodles for doneness, prick them with a fork.

Crockery Cooking

Dinner that cooks by itself is a dream come true with an electric crockery cooker, especially if you keep these points in mind:

● Crockery cookers are best for cooking less expensive cuts of meat because the long cooking on a low-heat setting makes these cuts tender. The low temperature also keeps the meat from shrinking.

● To start the cooker while you're away, plug your crockery cooker into an automatic timer. Just prepare the food ahead and chill it thoroughly. Then, before you leave, place the chilled food in the cooker and cover. Set the timer to start the cooker, making sure the food won't stand more than two hours before the cooker comes on.

● When you lift the cover of your cooker to stir, be sure to replace it immediately. You can lose as much as 20 degrees of heat in just two minutes with the lid off. A quick peek will cool the food only one or two degrees.

● Don't use the cooker as a storage container. Also, the cooker should not be placed in the refrigerator or used to reheat cold food.

● Sudden temperature changes can damage the ceramic liner of the cooker. Never put cold food or cold water into a hot cooker. Turn on the cooker only after foods are in the pot.

● Get extra mileage out of your cooker by using it as a serving container. For a buffet, place it right on the table and let guests help themselves. Or use it to keep a warm punch heated, or in place of a fondue pot or chafing dish.

● Make cleanup easy by adding warm water to the cooker just after removing the food. Never immerse the cord or cooker in water. If your cooker has a removable liner, remove it for easy washing.

Spicy Fruited Lamb

Preparation: 25 minutes
Cooking Time: 10 hours

4	lamb shanks, halved crosswise (about 3½ pounds total)
	Salt
	Pepper
¼	cup all-purpose flour
2	tablespoons cooking oil
½	cup dried apricots
½	cup pitted dried prunes, halved
½	cup raisins
¼	cup beef broth
2	tablespoons sugar
2	tablespoons vinegar
2	tablespoons lemon juice
½	teaspoon ground allspice
½	teaspoon ground cinnamon

● Sprinkle shanks with salt and pepper. Coat with flour. In a large skillet brown shanks in hot oil. Drain off fat.

In an electric crockery cooker combine fruits, broth, sugar, vinegar, lemon juice, and spices. Add shanks. Cover and cook on low-heat setting for 9 to 10 hours or till lamb is tender.

Dried fruit plumps up to its flavorful best when it cooks slow and easy with the lamb shanks in the crockery cooker.

1	tablespoon cornstarch
1	tablespoon cold water
	Hot cooked rice

● Remove shanks. Keep warm. Strain juices, reserving fruit. Skim fat from juices. Measure *1½ cups* juices, adding water. Transfer to a saucepan. Combine cornstarch and water. Stir into juices in saucepan. Cook and stir till thickened and bubbly. Stir in fruit. Heat through. Serve over lamb shanks and hot cooked rice. Makes 4 to 6 servings.

Vegetable-Beef Soup

Preparation: 10 minutes
Cooking Time: 1½ hours

1	pound beef stew meat, cut into 1-inch pieces
1	tablespoon cooking oil
4	cups water
1	16-ounce can tomatoes, cut up
1	8¾-ounce can whole kernel corn, drained
1	envelope *regular* onion soup mix
1	teaspoon sugar
⅛	teaspoon garlic powder
⅛	teaspoon pepper

● In a 4½-quart Dutch oven brown meat, half at a time, in hot oil for 4 to 5 minutes. Drain off fat.

Stir in water, *undrained* tomatoes, corn, soup mix, sugar, garlic powder, and pepper. Bring to boiling; reduce heat. Cover and simmer for 1 hour or till beef stew meat is tender.

Too much soup for a small family? Freeze it! Place half of the soup in a 1-quart freezer container. Seal, label, and freeze.

To reheat, transfer the frozen soup to a medium saucepan. Cover and cook over medium-low heat about 1 hour or till heated through, stirring often. Or, transfer the frozen soup to a 1½-quart nonmetal casserole. Micro-cook, uncovered, on 100% power (high) for 18 to 20 minutes, stirring every 6 minutes.

1	10-ounce package frozen mixed vegetables
1	cup frozen loose-pack hash brown potatoes

● Stir vegetables and potatoes into meat mixture in saucepan. Bring to boiling; reduce heat. Cover and simmer for 10 to 15 minutes more or till vegetables are crisp-tender. Makes 6 servings.

Take-It-Easy Menu

This stove-top meal goes together in minutes and simmers unattended to perfection. That way you'll have some time to relax before dinner.

MENU
Skillet Steak and Vegetables
Festive Fruit Salad
French bread

MENU COUNTDOWN
1 Hour Ahead
Prepare and assemble Skillet Steak and Vegetables.
45 Minutes Ahead
Simmer steak and vegetables on the stove top.
15 Minutes Ahead
Assemble Festive Fruit Salad.
Set out bread.

Festive Fruit Salad
(see recipe, page 62)

Skillet Steak and Vegetables
(see recipe, page 62)

Skillet Steak And Vegetables

Pictured on pages 60–61.

**Preparation: 15 minutes
Cooking Time: 45 minutes**

1 pound lean beef round
    steak, cut ½ inch thick
1 tablespoon cooking oil
1 10¼-ounce can beef gravy
¼ cup dry red wine
¾ teaspoon dried thyme,
    crushed
⅛ to ¼ teaspoon pepper

● Cut steak into 4 pieces. In a large skillet brown steak in hot oil. Drain off fat. In a bowl stir together gravy, wine, thyme, and pepper. Pour over steak.

With canned gravy, you don't have to thicken the juices once the meat and vegetables are cooked.

3 medium red potatoes,
    quartered
2 medium carrots, cut into
    1-inch pieces
1 medium onion, cut into
    8 wedges

● Arrange potatoes, carrots, and onion on meat in skillet. Bring to boiling; reduce heat. Cover and simmer about 45 minutes or till meat is tender. Transfer meat and vegetables to dinner plates. Spoon pan juices over. Makes 4 servings.

Festive Fruit Salad

Pictured on pages 60–61.

Total Time: 10 minutes

1 11-ounce can pineapple
    tidbits and mandarin
    orange sections, drained
1 kiwi fruit, peeled
    and sliced
    Lettuce leaves

● Arrange pineapple tidbits and orange sections and kiwi fruit on 4 lettuce-lined salad plates.

It may look fancy, but it's super simple to make. Assemble the fruits and dressing while the main dish bakes.

¼ cup mayonnaise *or* salad
    dressing
1 tablespoon milk
¼ cup broken walnuts

● In a small mixing bowl stir together mayonnaise or salad dressing and milk. Spoon over fruit mixture. Sprinkle with nuts. Makes 4 servings.

Hearty German Stew

Preparation: 30 minutes
Cooking Time: 1¾ hours

1 **pound beef stew meat, cut into 1-inch cubes**
2 **tablespoons cooking oil**
1 **medium onion, chopped**
1 **12-ounce can beer**
1 **cup water**
¼ **cup tomato paste**
1 **tablespoon paprika**
½ **teaspoon caraway seed**
¼ **teaspoon salt**
¼ **teaspoon pepper**

● In a large saucepan cook *half* of the meat in hot oil till meat is brown. Remove meat from saucepan. Repeat with remaining meat and onion. Drain off fat.

Return all meat to saucepan. Add the beer, water, tomato paste, paprika, caraway seed, salt, and pepper. Bring to boiling; reduce heat. Cover and simmer for 1 to 1¼ hours.

3 **medium potatoes**
1 **8-ounce can sauerkraut, rinsed and drained**
2 **tablespoons snipped parsley**

● Meanwhile, peel potatoes and cut into 1-inch pieces. Add potatoes, drained sauerkraut, and parsley to saucepan. Cover and cook about 25 minutes or till meat and vegetables are tender. Serves 4.

Microwave Method: In a 2-quart nonmetal casserole combine meat, onion, beer, *2 tablespoons* tomato paste, paprika, caraway seed, salt, and pepper. Stir in *only ½ cup* water. (Omit oil and the remaining 2 tablespoons tomato paste.) Micro-cook, uncovered, on 100% power (high) about 5 minutes or till bubbly. Stir. Cook, covered, on 50% power (medium) for 20 minutes. Stir in the potatoes, sauerkraut, and parsley. Cover and cook on medium about 30 minutes more or till meat and vegetables are tender, stirring every 10 minutes.

Brew in a stew? That's right, but don't expect to get tipsy from it. All the beer's alcohol evaporates during cooking, leaving just the subtle beer flavor.

Stop at the Deli

Stop at a neighborhood shop or supermarket deli to find oodles of goodies for a last-minute meal. With some imagination (and the recipes on the next four pages), you can dress up meats, cheeses, salads, and breads into dishes that look like you made them from scratch.

German-Style Ham Bake

Total Time: 30 minutes

6 ounces thinly sliced
   boiled ham
1 15½-ounce can German-
   style potato salad
1 8-ounce can sauerkraut,
   rinsed, drained, and
   snipped

● Cut ham into 1-inch-wide strips. Set aside. Combine potato salad and sauerkraut. Arrange *half* of ham strips in a 10x6x2-inch baking dish. Top with sauerkraut mixture.

4 ounces caraway *or* Swiss
   cheese, sliced

● Cover and bake in a 350° oven about 20 minutes or till heated through. Add remaining ham and cheese. Bake, uncovered, about 5 minutes more or till cheese melts. Makes 4 servings.

Microwave Method: Assemble as above. Micro-cook, loosely covered, on 100% power (high) for 3 to 4 minutes or till heated through, rotating dish a half-turn after 2 minutes. Add remaining ham and cheese. Cook, uncovered, for 2 to 3 minutes more or till cheese melts.

Guten Tag! This easy deli fix-up will help make your day a good one.

Smoked Turkey Sandwich

Total Time: 10 minutes

2 tablespoons mayonnaise
   or salad dressing
2 slices rye bread
3 *or* 4 spinach leaves
3 ounces thinly sliced
   smoked turkey breast
2 slices bacon, crisp cooked
   and drained
2 teaspoons crumbled blue
   cheese

● To assemble sandwich, spread the mayonnaise or salad dressing on both slices of bread. Top 1 slice of bread with spinach, turkey, bacon, and cheese. Top with remaining bread. Makes 1 serving.

What could be quicker: Add a bowl of hot soup to costar with this easy-to-fix sandwich.

Beef and Spinach Toss

Total Time: 25 minutes

1 6-ounce package frozen
   pea pods
5 ounces fresh spinach *or*
   mixed salad greens,
   torn (3 cups)
10 ounces cooked beef,
   cut into bite-size
   strips (2 cups)
1 small red onion, thinly
   sliced and separated
   into rings
1 cup cherry tomatoes

● In a colander run hot water over the pea pods about 1 minute or till thawed. Drain well. Set aside. Place spinach or salad greens in a large salad bowl. Add the pea pods, beef, onion, and tomatoes.

Cooked beef from the deli makes this no-fuss salad ultra-easy. If you have some leftover cooked beef at home, that works, too.

   Creamy Italian *or*
   buttermilk salad
   dressing
2 tablespoons crumbled
   blue cheese

● Pour salad dressing over spinach mixture, tossing lightly to coat. Sprinkle with the crumbled blue cheese. Serve immediately. Makes 4 servings.

Beef-Tostada Salads

Total Time: 30 minutes

3 8-inch tortillas

● Place tortillas in a single layer on a large baking sheet, overlapping as little as possible. Bake in a 350° oven for 10 to 15 minutes or till crisp.

Attention clock-watchers: Bypass the baked tortillas and serve this stacked salad over crisp flatbread wafers instead.

6 ounces thinly sliced
   cooked beef, chopped
1 pint three-bean salad, *or*
   one 17-ounce can three-
   bean salad, drained
   Shredded lettuce *or*
   alfalfa sprouts
   Shredded cheddar cheese
   Desired salad dressing

● Place tortillas on 3 dinner plates. Layer with beef, three-bean salad, lettuce or alfalfa sprouts, and cheese. Pass salad dressing. Makes 3 servings.

Nutty Cheese Fondue

Total Time: 35 minutes

12 ounces process Swiss cheese, shredded (3 cups)
2 tablespoons all-purpose flour
1 clove garlic, halved
1¼ cups dry white wine
1 tablespoon kirsch *or* dry sherry (optional)
Dash ground red pepper

2 tablespoons chopped nuts *or* sunflower nuts
1 loaf unsliced French, rye, *or* whole wheat bread, cubed

● In a medium bowl toss together cheese and flour. Rub the inside of a fondue pot with garlic. Discard garlic.

In a medium saucepan heat wine over medium heat till small bubbles rise to the surface. Stir in cheese mixture little by little, making sure cheese has melted before adding more. (Stir constantly and continue to add cheese till all is mixed in.) Stir till cheese mixture bubbles gently. Stir in kirsch, if desired, and red pepper.

● Pour cheese mixture into fondue pot. Keep cheese mixture bubbling gently over fondue burner. Sprinkle with nuts. Serve with bread cubes. Serves 4 to 6.

Fondue comes from the French word meaning "to melt." And this pot of creamy hot cheese is sure to melt in your mouth.

If you have individual slices of process Swiss cheese, just tear the slices into small pieces.

Easiest-Ever Gazpacho

Total Time: 15 minutes

½ pint marinated mixed
  vegetable salad
1 12-ounce can vegetable
  juice cocktail *or* hot-
  style vegetable juice
  cocktail
  Croutons

● Cut up any large vegetables. In a bowl stir together *undrained* vegetable salad and juice. Cover and chill in the freezer for 5 to 10 minutes. Serve with croutons. Makes 3 servings.

This soup lives up to its name. At the deli, choose a marinated cucumber mixture for more of a gazpacho flavor.

Seafood-Slaw Toss

Total Time: 20 minutes

8 ounces frozen salad-style,
  crab-flavored fish, *or*
  two 4½-ounce cans
  shrimp, rinsed and
  drained
½ pint creamy coleslaw
1 medium tomato, seeded
  and chopped
1 4-ounce can diced green
  chili peppers, drained

● Run cool water over fish about 5 minutes or till partially thawed. In a medium mixing bowl stir together fish or shrimp, coleslaw, tomato, and green chili peppers. Cover and chill in the freezer for 10 minutes.

It may not be the real McCoy, but crab-flavored fish is an inexpensive, low-cholesterol, and low-calorie substitute for crab.

By the time you get the frozen fish home from the store, it may already be partially thawed. In that case, use it right away without running it under cool water.

  Lettuce leaves
½ cup shredded Swiss *or*
  mozzarella cheese
  (2 ounces)

● Spoon fish mixture onto lettuce-lined plates. Sprinkle with cheese. Serves 4.

Ham Sandwich Packages

Preparation: 25 minutes
Baking Time: 20 minutes

 1 **10-ounce package**
       refrigerated hot loaf
 1 **3-ounce package cream**
       cheese with chives,
       cut up
1½ **cups chopped fully**
       cooked ham *or* ground
       fully cooked ham
       (8 ounces)
 1 **8-ounce can sauerkraut,**
       rinsed and well drained
 ¼ **cup chopped celery *or***
       green pepper
 1 **green onion, sliced**

       Milk
 ½ **teaspoon caraway seed**

● Cut hot loaf dough into 8 portions. Cover and set aside.

   For filling, in a mixing bowl use a wooden spoon to stir cream cheese till softened. Stir in ham, sauerkraut, celery or green pepper, and onion.

● On a lightly floured surface roll each portion of dough into a 5-inch circle. Spoon the filling onto the centers of *half* of the circles (see photo, top right). Place remaining circles on top. Seal.

● Place the 4 filled sandwich packages on a greased baking sheet. Brush tops lightly with milk. Sprinkle with caraway seed. Prick tops. Bake in a 375° oven for 15 to 20 minutes or till golden brown. Remove from baking sheet. Cool slightly on a wire rack (see photo, bottom right). Serve warm immediately or chill overnight. Makes 4 servings.

● For *each* serving, in the morning pack *1 chilled* sandwich in an insulated lunch box with a frozen ice pack.

Spoon the ham mixture onto the centers of four circles of dough. Place the remaining dough circles on top. Seal the edges using the tines of a fork, or pinch with your fingertips.

Bake the sandwich packages in a 375° oven for 15 to 20 minutes or till the dough is golden brown. Transfer to a wire rack with a spatula.

Turkey Reuben

Total Time: 10 minutes

1 tablespoon mayonnaise *or* salad dressing
2 slices rye bread
2 ounces thinly sliced cooked turkey breast
¼ cup sauerkraut, well drained
1½ ounces sliced Monterey Jack cheese

● Spread mayonnaise or salad dressing on both slices of bread. Place sliced turkey on 1 bread slice. Top with sauerkraut. Place sliced cheese on sauerkraut, then top with remaining slice of bread. Cover and chill overnight. Makes 1 serving.
   In the morning pack the *chilled* sandwich in an insulated lunch box with a frozen ice pack.

Pick up cooked turkey breast either at a delicatessen or your grocer's meat case.

Fruity Chicken Sandwiches

Total Time: 15 minutes

¼ cup plain yogurt
1 tablespoon Dijon-style mustard
  Dash ground allspice
1 8¼-ounce can crushed pineapple, well drained, *or* 1 small tart apple, chopped
1 5-ounce can chunk-style chicken, drained and chopped
¼ cup raisins *or* chopped walnuts

● In a medium mixing bowl stir together yogurt, mustard, and allspice. Stir in pineapple or apple, chicken, and raisins or walnuts. Cover and chill overnight. Makes 4 servings.

You've got several delicious possibilities. Combine the chicken mixture with pineapple or apples and with raisins or walnuts. Or invent your own nutty fruit combo.

Lettuce leaves
8 slices whole wheat bread

● For *each* serving, in the morning pack *2* slices of bread and *1* lettuce leaf in separate small clear plastic bags. Carry with *1 portion* of the *chilled* chicken mixture in an insulated lunch box with an ice pack.
   At lunchtime, assemble bread, lettuce, and chicken mixture into a sandwich.

Yogurt Mania

Let your imagination run wild! Listed below are different kinds of yogurts, fruits, crunchies, and extras you can choose from to customize your own carton of yogurt. A delicious way to start is with the editors' choices listed on the opposite page. Then try your own zany combinations. You're sure to enjoy the tinkering as well as the tasting. We certainly did!

Yogurt	Fruit	Crunchies	Extras
Blueberry	Apples	Almond brickle pieces	Chopped dates
Coffee	Bananas	Almonds	Cooked wheat berries
Lemon	Berries	Chow mein noodles	Cranberry-orange relish
Orange	Dried fruit bits	Granola	Jams and jellies
Peach	Grapes	Grape-Nuts cereal	Peanut butter
Plain	Kiwi fruit	Peanuts	Semisweet chocolate pieces
Raspberry	Melon	Pecans	Shredded lemon or orange peel
Strawberry	Oranges	Pumpkin seeds	Sweetened and flavored coffee powder
Vanilla	Peaches	Sunflower nuts	Toasted coconut
	Pears	Sweetened bran cereal	Toasted wheat germ
	Pineapple	Walnuts	
	Plums		
	Raisins		

Editors' Choices

1. Vanilla yogurt, granola, pecans, and chopped apple
2. Strawberry yogurt, sliced banana, and Grape-Nuts cereal
3. Vanilla yogurt, semisweet chocolate pieces, and almond brickle pieces
4. Lemon yogurt, granola, and chopped banana
5. Vanilla yogurt, raspberry preserves, and orange marmalade
6. Vanilla yogurt and chopped plums
7. Blueberry yogurt and chopped peaches
8. Peach yogurt and toasted wheat germ
9. Blueberry yogurt and chopped bananas
10. Vanilla yogurt, kiwi fruit, and toasted sliced almonds
11. Lemon yogurt, blueberries, and toasted slivered almonds
12. Raspberry yogurt and cooked wheat berries
13. Strawberry yogurt and sliced strawberries
14. Lemon yogurt, melon balls, and toasted coconut
15. Vanilla yogurt, peanut butter, and semisweet chocolate pieces

Tortilla-Beef Roll-Ups

Preparation: 10 minutes

4 11- *or* 12-inch flour
   tortillas
1 8-ounce container sour
   cream dip with bacon
   and horseradish
10 to 12 ounces thinly sliced
   cooked beef
   Lettuce leaves

● Spread *1* side of *each* tortilla with about *2* *tablespoons* of the horseradish dip, covering whole tortilla. Top with *1* or *2 slices* of beef. Spread with another *2 tablespoons* of the dip. Top with lettuce leaves. Roll up tortillas jelly-roll style. Halve crosswise. Wrap in clear plastic wrap. Chill overnight. Serves 4.

● For *each* serving, in the morning pack *2 chilled* roll-up halves in an insulated lunch box with a frozen ice pack.

Count 'em! Only four ingredients make up this quick-as-a-wink sandwich.

Brown-Bag Safety Tips

There's more to toting your lunch than tossing food in a bag. Follow our simple suggestions to keep your lunch safe and fresh tasting for hours.

● When you prepare lunch, make sure anything that touches the food is clean.

● Seal foods in clean airtight containers or plastic storage bags.

● If you want lettuce or sliced tomato on your sandwich, pack it separately in a clear plastic bag and assemble the sandwich at lunchtime.

● Chill cold foods overnight. Then, in the morning, pack them in prechilled thermoses or in insulated lunch boxes with an ice pack.

● Use new lunch bags or clean lunch boxes.

● Keep your lunch in a cool dry place all morning.

● If you can, store your lunch in a refrigerator.

Egg Salad Sandwiches

Preparation: 35 minutes

4 eggs
⅓ cup mayonnaise *or* salad dressing
½ teaspoon prepared mustard
⅛ teaspoon garlic salt

● Place eggs in a saucepan. Add enough water to cover eggs. Bring to boiling; reduce heat. Cover and simmer for 15 minutes. Drain. Fill saucepan with cold water. Let stand at least 2 minutes.
  Meanwhile, in a bowl combine mayonnaise or salad dressing, mustard, and garlic salt. Drain, peel, and chop eggs. Stir into mayonnaise mixture.

1 4-ounce package shredded cheddar cheese (1 cup)
¼ cup seeded and finely chopped cucumber
1 green onion, sliced

● Stir cheese, cucumber, and onion into mayonnaise mixture in bowl. Cover and chill. Makes 4 servings.

2 pita bread rounds, halved crosswise
Lettuce leaves

● For *each* serving, in the morning pack *1* pita half and *1* lettuce leaf in separate small clear plastic bags. Carry with *1 portion* of the *chilled* egg mixture in an insulated lunch box with an ice pack.
  At lunchtime, line the pita pocket with lettuce. Spoon in egg mixture.

A tasty spin-off of the old standby. We've added cucumber and cheese and packed the salad in a pita.

Marinated Cheese Salad

Preparation: 15 minutes

6 ounces Colby, Edam, Gouda, Jarlsberg, Monterey Jack, *or* Swiss cheese, cubed
1 cup sliced fresh mushrooms
1 cup cherry tomatoes, halved
1 cup broccoli flowerets
⅓ cup Italian salad dressing

● In a medium mixing bowl combine cheese, mushrooms, tomatoes, and broccoli. Drizzle with salad dressing, tossing to coat. Chill several hours or overnight, stirring occasionally. Serves 2.

● For *each* serving, in the morning pack *1 chilled* portion in an insulated lunch box with a frozen ice pack.

Savor a salad for lunch. This one is loaded with cheese, mushrooms, tomatoes, and broccoli.

Bran-Nut Refrigerator Muffins

Preparation: 15 minutes
Baking Time: 20 minutes

1½ cups all-purpose flour 1 cup unprocessed wheat bran 2½ teaspoons baking powder ¾ teaspoon ground cinnamon ¼ teaspoon salt ¼ teaspoon ground nutmeg	● In a large mixing bowl stir together flour, bran, baking powder, cinnamon, salt, and nutmeg.	This batter keeps in the refrigerator up to seven days, so go ahead and make just a few muffins at a time.
2 beaten eggs ¾ cup milk ⅓ cup packed brown sugar ⅓ cup cooking oil 1 teaspoon finely shredded lemon *or* orange peel ⅓ cup sunflower nuts	● In a bowl combine eggs, milk, brown sugar, cooking oil, and lemon or orange peel. Add to flour mixture. Stir just till moistened (batter will be thick). Fold in sunflower nuts. Store in a covered container in the refrigerator up to 7 days.	For a nifty way to bake one or two muffins, use your microwave oven. Line one or two 6-ounce custard cups with a paper bake cup. Spoon about 3 tablespoons batter into each. For one muffin, micro-cook on 100% power (high) for 30 to 60 seconds. For two muffins, cook on high for 1 to 1¼ minutes.
	● To bake, gently stir batter. Grease desired number of muffin pans or line with paper bake cups. Fill ⅔ full. Bake in a 400° oven for 15 to 18 minutes or till done. Makes up to 12 muffins.	
	● **Apple-Raisin Muffins:** Prepare Bran-Nut Refrigerator Muffins as above, *except* pour *boiling water* over ½ cup snipped *dried apple*. Let stand for 5 minutes. Drain well. Add apple and ¼ cup *raisins* to batter with sunflower nuts.	You'll have a tough time choosing between the bran-nut, apple-raisin, date-nut, and jelly versions of these healthful muffins.
	● **Date-Nut Muffins:** Prepare Bran-Nut Refrigerator Muffins as above, *except* substitute ⅓ cup chopped *walnuts or pecans* for the sunflower nuts. Fold the nuts and ⅔ cup coarsely chopped pitted *dates* into batter.	
	● **Jelly Muffins:** Prepare Bran-Nut Refrigerator Muffins as above, *except,* for each muffin, spoon about *1 tablespoon* batter into muffin cup. Make a slight indentation into the center. Spoon ½ teaspoon *jelly* into indentation. Top with *2 tablespoons* batter.	

Nutty Orange Pancakes

Total Time: 30 minutes

½ cup maple-flavored syrup
½ teaspoon finely shredded orange peel

● In a small saucepan heat syrup and orange peel over low heat till warm.

1 beaten egg
½ cup orange juice
2 tablespoons brown sugar
1 cup packaged biscuit mix
¼ cup chopped walnuts *or* pecans

● Meanwhile, for pancakes, in a medium bowl combine egg, orange juice, and sugar. Beat with a fork till well combined. Add biscuit mix. Beat with a fork till nearly smooth. Stir in nuts.

Butter *or* margarine

● Pour a scant ¼ *cup* batter onto a hot lightly greased griddle or heavy skillet. Cook over medium-low heat for 1 to 2 minutes per side or till golden brown (see photo, below). Repeat with remaining batter. Serve with butter or margarine and warm maple syrup mixture. Cover and chill any remaining syrup mixture. Makes 8 pancakes.

Luscious pancakes that are quick enough for a busy morning breakfast and special enough for a leisurely brunch.

Spoon the batter onto a hot lightly greased griddle or heavy skillet. Turn the pancakes when they have a bubbly surface and slightly dry edges. This should take about 1 to 2 minutes per side.

Quick Fruit Waffles

Total Time: 10 minutes

1 teaspoon sugar
  Dash ground cinnamon
2 frozen waffles
  Butter *or* margarine

● In a small bowl stir together sugar and cinnamon. Toast waffles according to package directions. Spread lightly with butter or margarine. Sprinkle lightly with sugar-cinnamon mixture.

Dairy sour cream *or* vanilla yogurt
  Desired fruit (blueberries; sliced strawberries, bananas, nectarines, *or* peaches; *or* drained canned fruit)

● Spread some sour cream or yogurt on the centers of the waffles. Top with fruit. Makes 1 serving.

Every member of our taste panel agreed: This breakfast is a great way to get on the road in the morning, especially with the frozen waffle shortcut.

Breakfast Melon

Total Time: 10 minutes

½ cup cream-style cottage cheese
2 tablespoons mixed dried fruit bits
2 tablespoons lemon *or* peach yogurt
¼ cantaloupe *or* honeydew melon

● In a small mixing bowl stir together cottage cheese, fruit bits, and yogurt. Place melon on a serving plate.

1 tablespoon granola

● Spoon cottage cheese mixture over melon. Sprinkle with granola. Serves 1.

For a unique breakfast on the run, omit melon quarters and spoon the cottage cheese mixture into an ice cream cone.

Pita Scramble

Total Time: 15 minutes

3 eggs
3 tablespoons milk
1 2-ounce can mushroom stems and pieces, drained
1 tablespoon snipped parsley
⅛ teaspoon onion powder
⅛ teaspoon dried basil, crushed
Dash pepper

● In a medium mixing bowl beat together eggs and milk. Stir in mushrooms, parsley, onion powder, basil, and pepper.

1 tablespoon butter *or* margarine
¼ cup shredded cheddar cheese (1 ounce)
1 pita bread round, halved crosswise

● In a medium skillet melt butter or margarine over medium heat. Pour in egg mixture. Cook without stirring till mixture begins to set on the bottom and around edges. Lift and fold partially cooked eggs so uncooked portion flows underneath. Continue cooking till eggs are cooked throughout but still glossy and moist. Sprinkle with cheese. Allow cheese to melt slightly. Spoon into pita halves. Makes 2 servings.

Symptom: Early morning stomach growls.

Prescription: Scrambled eggs bursting with mushrooms, parsley, spices, and cheese.

Directions: Pack it in a pita.

Dose: Once in the morning before work or school.

Microwave Omelet In a Cup

Enjoy breakfast minus any cleanup. Micro-cook an omelet in a disposable paper cup and take it with you. (A microwave-safe coffee cup will work, too.)

In a bowl beat together 1 *egg* and 1 tablespoon *milk*. Pour into a 9-ounce paper cup (without wax coating). Stir in 1 tablespoon shredded *cheddar cheese* and dash *pepper*.

Micro-cook, uncovered, on 100% power (high) for 50 to 90 seconds, stirring after 30 seconds. (When done, eggs should be soft-set and creamy.) Sprinkle with 1 tablespoon shredded *cheddar cheese*. Serves 1.

Cheese, Fruit, And Nut Spread

Total Time: 5 minutes

1	8-ounce container soft-style cream cheese
3	tablespoons milk
1	teaspoon lemon juice
¼	teaspoon ground allspice

● In a mixing bowl stir together cream cheese and milk till smooth. Stir in lemon juice and allspice.

¼	cup mixed dried fruit, chopped
¼	cup finely chopped walnuts

● Stir in dried fruit and nuts. Store, tightly covered, in the refrigerator up to 1 week. Serve on quick bread, muffins, bagels, or toast. Makes 1½ cups.

A dab of this spread on bread will keep hunger pangs away all morning.

Is 1½ cups too much? Then freeze some for later. Just spoon the spread into a freezer container. Seal, label, and freeze up to 3 months. Thaw at room temperature for 2½ to 3 hours or in the refrigerator overnight.

Orange Breakfast Nog

Total Time: 10 minutes

1½	cups buttermilk
3	eggs
½	of a 6-ounce can (⅓ cup) frozen orange juice concentrate
2	tablespoons brown sugar
½	teaspoon vanilla

● In a blender container combine buttermilk, eggs, orange juice concentrate, brown sugar, and vanilla. Cover and blend till smooth.

2	large ice cubes

● Add ice cubes. Cover and blend till smooth and frothy. Makes 3 servings.

Open your eyes with this refreshing breakfast in a glass.

TODAY
9:30 Call John
10:00 Appt. w/

Canadian Bacon Kabobs

Preparation: 15 minutes
Cooking Time: 5 minutes

1 **11-ounce can mandarin orange sections**
1 **8¼-ounce can pineapple chunks (juice pack)**
6 **slices Canadian-style bacon**

● Drain the mandarin oranges and pineapple chunks, reserving juice. Roll up bacon slices. Alternately thread bacon, oranges, and pineapple on two 10-inch skewers. Cover and chill the extra fruit. Place kabobs in a 12x7½x2-inch baking dish. Pour reserved fruit juice over kabobs. Cover and refrigerate overnight.

Say good morning to skewers full of Canadian-style bacon and luscious fruit. Add a couple of bagels and cream cheese and you've got a great breakfast in minutes.

Vanilla yogurt (optional)
Nutmeg (optional)

● To serve, drain off juice from kabobs. Broil kabobs 3 to 4 inches from the heat about 5 minutes or till edges of bacon are brown and fruit is warm. Top the remaining fruit with vanilla yogurt and nutmeg, if desired. Makes 2 servings.

To make four servings, just double the meat and use the extra fruit to fill four skewers.

Wheat 'n' Cheese Oven-Fried Chicken

Baking Time: 50 minutes

20 **wheat wafers**
¼ **cup grated Parmesan cheese**

● Turn oven to 375°. Put the wheat wafers in a plastic bag. Close the bag. Use a rolling pin to crush the wafers. Add the cheese. Close the bag. Shake gently to mix crumbs and cheese. Pour into a pie plate.

2 **whole medium chicken breasts, halved lengthwise**
2 **tablespoons butter *or* margarine**
1 **teaspoon Worcestershire sauce**

● Rinse chicken under cold water. Pat dry with paper towels. Put butter or margarine into a small saucepan. Place saucepan over burner. Turn burner to low heat. When butter or margarine melts, turn off burner. Take saucepan off burner. Add Worcestershire sauce to saucepan. Stir till mixed.

● Using a pastry brush, brush chicken on all sides with butter mixture. Roll each chicken piece in crumb mixture till coated. Arrange chicken pieces, skin sides up, in a 12x7½x2-inch baking dish so pieces don't touch. Sprinkle any extra crumb mixture over chicken.

Put the baking dish into the hot oven. Bake about 50 minutes or till chicken is tender. Do not turn the chicken pieces. Makes 4 servings.

Get ready, kids, for a big hug when the family comes home to this crispy chicken dish. Renee and Jonathan, two of the kids who tested the recipe, gave it a 10 (the highest rating) for flavor.

Hammed-Up Pasta Primavera

Cooking Time: 20 minutes

6 cups water 5 ounces spaghetti	● Measure water. Pour into a large saucepan. Put pan on burner. Turn burner to high heat. When water boils, add spaghetti a little at a time. Cook for 10 to 12 minutes or till just tender.
1 10-ounce package frozen broccoli in cheese sauce 1 6-ounce package sliced fully cooked ham	● Meanwhile, in a saucepan cook vegetables according to package directions. On a cutting board use a sharp knife to cut the ham into bite-size pieces. Stir ham into the hot vegetables in saucepan. Heat through. Remove saucepan from heat.
2 tablespoons butter *or* margarine Grated Parmesan cheese (optional)	● Place a colander in the sink. With adult help, carefully pour spaghetti and water into colander. Let spaghetti stand for a few minutes to drain well. Return spaghetti to saucepan. Use a rubber scraper to stir butter or margarine into hot spaghetti till it melts. Arrange spaghetti on a serving platter. Carefully spoon broccoli mixture over spaghetti. Sprinkle with Parmesan cheese, if you like. Makes 3 servings.

You should have seen our taste-testing kids dig into this one. They were all members of the clean plate club! Jason even asked for a copy of the recipe so he could make it at home.

Hey, kids, don't try to be musclemen. If the pot of spaghetti is too heavy for you to lift, let Mom or Dad wrestle with it.

Kids in the Kitchen

In every busy family, a little teamwork goes a long way, especially in meal preparation. So let your kids pitch in and take charge of the kitchen once in a while. The kid-tested recipes on pages 84 to 89 are a great place for your young chef to begin.

Each of these detailed recipes can be started by kids (10 years or older) after school and be ready to be enjoyed shortly after the rest of the family comes home. Kids will jump at the chance to make dinner, especially if you let them get out of doing the dishes!

Baked Potato Bonanza

Baking Time: 60 minutes

3 medium baking potatoes (about 1 pound total)	● Turn the oven to 425°. Scrub the potatoes thoroughly with a vegetable brush. Prick potatoes with a fork. Place potatoes on oven rack in hot oven. Bake for 40 to 60 minutes or till soft when squeezed with a towel.	Bake the potatoes lickety-split in a microwave oven. Start the potatoes about 25 minutes before your family is ready to eat. Prick the potatoes with a fork and put them in a shallow nonmetal baking dish. Micro-cook, uncovered, on 100% power (high) for 7 minutes. Turn the potatoes and cook on high for 7 to 10 minutes more. Let stand for 5 minutes.
1 frankfurter 1 medium green onion 2 ounces cheddar cheese	● Meanwhile, prepare toppings for potatoes. On a cutting board use a sharp knife to cut the frankfurter into thin, round slices. On the same board use the knife to trim the roots and ends of the green onion. Pull off any withered leaves. Cut the onion into thin slices. Put waxed paper under cheese shredder to catch the cheese. Hold the shredder with one hand and move the cheese down across the shredder.	
Butter *or* margarine Cottage cheese *or* softened cream cheese Dairy sour cream *or* plain yogurt Bottled barbecue sauce *or* taco sauce Sunflower nuts Salt Pepper	● To serve, cut a cross in the top of each baked potato. Set out butter or margarine, cottage cheese or cream cheese, sour cream or yogurt, barbecue or taco sauce, sunflower nuts, salt, pepper, shredded cheese, frankfurter slices, and green onion. Top potatoes any way you like. Serves 3.	

Easy Pot Roast And Gravy

Cooking Time: 2¼ hours

1 3- to 4-pound beef chuck
   pot roast
⅔ cup vegetable juice
   cocktail
1 envelope instant meat
   marinade mix
8 whole new potatoes
3 medium carrots
3 stalks celery
2 medium onions

● Use a sharp knife to trim fat from the pot roast. Discard fat. In a Dutch oven stir together vegetable juice cocktail and marinade mix. Place meat in marinade mixture. Let stand for 15 minutes, turning meat once.

   Scrub potatoes and carrots. On a cutting board use a sharp knife to cut carrots into 1-inch pieces. Cut celery into 1-inch pieces. Peel onions; cut into wedges. Place onions in Dutch oven with meat. Set potatoes, carrots, and celery aside.

● Place Dutch oven over burner. Turn burner to high heat. When liquid boils, turn burner to low heat till liquid bubbles gently. Cover and cook for 40 minutes. Add potatoes, carrots, and celery. Cover and cook for 1¼ to 1½ hours more or till meat and vegetables are tender.

● With adult help, remove Dutch oven from burner. Transfer roast and vegetables to a serving platter. Cover with foil to keep warm. For gravy, pour juices from Dutch oven into a 2-cup measure. Spoon off as much fat as possible. Add water, if necessary, to equal 1½ cups.

½ cup cold water
2 tablespoons all-purpose
   flour

● In a screw-top jar combine water and flour. Screw the lid onto the jar tightly. Shake the jar till water and flour are well mixed. Pour pan juices and flour mixture in Dutch oven. Place on burner. Turn burner to medium heat. Cook and stir till thickened and bubbly. Cook and stir 1 minute more. Spoon some gravy over vegetables and meat. Pass remaining gravy. Makes 6 to 8 servings.

We'd like to pass on some words of wisdom from Andy, one of the kids who made this recipe in our Test Kitchen: "Wear a gas mask when you cut the onions!"

Recipe-testers Andy and Pam said they thought it would be a good idea to wait for adult help when it's time to make gravy.

Bacon-Topped Beef Bundles

Baking Time: 35 minutes

1 egg
⅓ cup quick-cooking rolled oats
⅓ cup milk
1 single-serving envelope *instant* onion soup mix
1 pound ground beef

● Turn the oven to 350°. Crack the egg on the side of a large mixing bowl. Working over the bowl, gently separate the eggshell halves and pour the egg into the bowl. Use a fork to gently beat the egg to mix the yolk and white.

Add oats and milk to the bowl with the egg. Add soup mix. Stir with a fork to mix well. Use your hands to crumble the meat into the bowl. Mix the meat and egg mixture together.

Our kid testers thought these deserved a more glamorous title. They called them "Meat Loaves à la Bacon."

2 slices bacon, halved crosswise

● Separate bacon slices and place side by side in a medium skillet. Place skillet over burner. Turn burner to medium-low heat. Cook bacon for 5 to 6 minutes or till nearly done. Turn off burner. Use tongs to remove bacon from skillet. Put bacon on paper towels to drain and cool.

Pat meat mixture into an 8x3-inch rectangle. Cut into 4 equal portions (see photo, right).

● When bacon is cool enough to handle, place 1 piece on each portion of meat, pressing in slightly. Place meat in a 12x7½x2-inch baking dish. Bake in the hot oven for 30 to 35 minutes or till meat is done and bacon is crisp.

Use your hands to shape the meat mixture into an 8x3-inch rectangle. If necessary, use a ruler to measure the rectangle. Use a metal spatula or kitchen knife to cut meat into four equal parts.

Catsup
Mustard
Pickles
Tomato slices

● Use hot pads to remove dish from oven. Use a pancake turner to remove meat from dish. Drain meat on paper towels. Serve with catsup, mustard, pickles, and tomatoes. Makes 4 servings.

Sherry Cheese Log
(see recipe, page 93)

Crab-Havarti Pastries
(see recipe, page 93)

Tortilla Chip Bites

Total Time: 20 minutes

1 10½-ounce can bean dip
2 tablespoons taco sauce
32 round tortilla chips
1 cup shredded lettuce
1 cup shredded cheddar *or*
Monterey Jack cheese
(4 ounces)
Taco sauce

● In a bowl stir together bean dip and 2 tablespoons taco sauce. Spread bean mixture onto *half* of the tortilla chips. Sprinkle bean mixture with lettuce and cheese. Top with remaining tortilla chips to make sandwiches. Serve with additional taco sauce. Makes 16.

Phyllo-Spinach Squares

Preparation: 35 minutes
Baking Time: 30 minutes

2 **12-ounce packages frozen spinach soufflé**
12 **sheets frozen phyllo dough (18x14-inch rectangles), thawed**
½ **cup butter *or* margarine, melted**

● Thaw frozen soufflé by placing containers in plastic bags. Seal tightly. Place in a bowl of hot water for 15 minutes, changing water twice. (Or, remove soufflé from foil tray and place in a microwave-safe mixing bowl. Micro-cook, uncovered, on 30% power [medium-low] for 5 minutes. Break up soufflé with a fork. Cook for 5 to 7 minutes more or till soufflé is thawed, stirring once.)

Meanwhile, arrange *half* of the phyllo dough in the bottom of a 15x10x1-inch baking pan, brushing melted butter or margarine between each sheet. (Allow edges of dough to overlap sides of pan.)

Look for phyllo dough in your grocer's freezer. Thaw the phyllo dough in the refrigerator overnight or according to package directions.

1 **8-ounce can sliced water chestnuts, drained**

● Spread soufflé mixture evenly over dough (see photo, right). Top with water chestnuts and remaining phyllo dough, brushing butter or margarine between each sheet. Fold edges of phyllo dough toward center. Brush with remaining butter or margarine. Score top layers of phyllo dough into 48 squares. If desired, cover and chill till ready to bake.

● Bake, uncovered, in a 400° oven for 25 to 30 minutes or till golden brown. Cool slightly. Cut through all layers. Serve warm. Makes 48.

Spread the thawed soufflé mixture evenly over the first six layers of phyllo.

Crab-Havarti Pastries

Pictured on pages 90–91.

Preparation: 30 minutes
Baking Time: 30 minutes

1	**15-ounce package folded refrigerated unbaked piecrusts (2 crusts)**

● Let piecrusts stand at room temperature for 10 to 15 minutes according to package directions. (Or, remove piecrusts from pouch. Micro-cook on 30% power [medium-low] about 45 seconds.) Unfold piecrusts. Place piecrusts on an ungreased baking sheet.

We should call these "Abracadabra Pastries." They did a remarkable disappearing act when we made them in our Test Kitchen. We guarantee the same results when you set them out for your guests.

1	**large onion, chopped**
2	**cloves garlic, minced**
2	**tablespoons cooking oil**
1	**tablespoon all-purpose flour**
⅓	**cup milk**
1	**cup shredded havarti cheese (4 ounces)**
1	**6-ounce can crabmeat, drained, flaked, and cartilage removed**
¼	**cup snipped parsley**

● Meanwhile, in a saucepan cook onion and garlic in oil till onion is tender but not brown. Stir in flour. Add milk all at once. Cook and stir till thickened and bubbly. Cook and stir 1 minute more. Add cheese. Stir till it melts. Remove from heat. Stir in crab and parsley.

Milk
Parsley (optional)

● Spoon *half* of the crab mixture onto half of *each* piecrust. Moisten edges with water. Fold piecrusts in half; turn edges under. Seal edges with tines of a fork.
   Prick tops of pastries and brush with milk. Bake in a 375° oven for 25 to 30 minutes or till pastry is brown. Garnish with parsley, if desired. Makes 2.

Sherry Cheese Spread

Pictured on pages 90–91.

Preparation: 20 minutes

1	**8-ounce package cream cheese, cut up**
1½	**cups shredded Swiss cheese (6 ounces)**
3	**tablespoons milk**
2	**tablespoons dry *or* cream sherry**
1	**tablespoon snipped parsley**
	Assorted crackers

● In a small mixer bowl combine cream cheese and Swiss cheese. Set bowl in hot water for 15 minutes or till cheese is softened, stirring cheese and changing water once. Add milk, sherry, and parsley. Beat with an electric mixer till well combined. Serve with crackers. Makes 1¾ cups spread.

● **Sherry Cheese Logs:** Prepare Sherry Cheese Spread as above, *except* chill mixture in the freezer about 20 minutes or till firm enough to handle. Mold into two 6-inch-long logs. Coat the logs with sliced *toasted almonds*. Wrap in clear plastic wrap and refrigerate several hours or overnight. Serve with crackers. Makes 2 logs.

For even less hassle at party time, make and freeze the cheese logs ahead. Simply seal them in moisture- and vaporproof wrap, label, and freeze up to 2 months. Thaw the frozen logs for 2 hours at room temperature or overnight in the refrigerator.

Spinach Nuggets

Total Time: 25 minutes

2 10-ounce packages frozen chopped spinach
1 tablespoon dried minced onion

● In a saucepan cook the spinach and dried onion according to spinach package directions. Drain well.

Be prepared. These go like wildfire!

3 tablespoons butter *or* margarine
1 cup herb-seasoned stuffing mix
1 cup grated Parmesan cheese
2 beaten eggs

● In a mixing bowl stir together hot spinach mixture and butter or margarine till butter melts. Add stuffing mix and cheese. Stir in eggs. Shape into 1-inch balls. (If desired, place spinach balls in a shallow pan. Cover and freeze about 1 hour or till firm. Transfer spinach balls to freezer containers. Seal, label, and freeze up to 4 months.)

To make handling the mixture easier, drop small mounds onto a baking sheet lined with waxed paper. Freeze about 10 minutes, then shape the mounds into balls.

● Place *unfrozen* spinach balls on a greased baking sheet. Bake in a 375° oven about 7 minutes or till heated through. (Or, place *frozen* spinach balls in a shallow baking pan. Bake in a 375° oven for 15 to 20 minutes or till heated through.) Makes about 48.

Microwave Method: Place frozen spinach and dried onion in a 1-quart nonmetal casserole with 2 tablespoons *water*. Micro-cook, covered, on 100% power (high) for 9 to 11 minutes, stirring once. Let stand 3 minutes. Drain well.

In the same casserole stir together hot spinach mixture and butter or margarine till butter melts. Add stuffing mix and Parmesan cheese. Stir in eggs. Shape as above. Freeze, if desired.

Place *half* of the spinach balls in a 12x7½x2-inch nonmetal baking dish. Cook *unfrozen* balls, uncovered, on 100% power (high) for 2 to 3 minutes or till heated through. Repeat with remaining balls. (Or, cook *frozen* spinach balls, uncovered, for 3 to 4 minutes.)

Index